G. K. CHESTERTON

Essential Writings

Selected
with an Introduction by
WILLIAM GRIFFIN

ORBIS BOOKS

Maryknoll, New York 10545

Founded in 1970, Orbis Books endeavors to publish works that enlighten the mind, nourish the spirit, and challenge the conscience. The publishing arm of the Maryknoll Fathers and Brothers, Orbis seeks to explore the global dimensions of the Christian faith and mission, to invite dialogue with diverse cultures and religious traditions, and to serve the cause of reconciliation and peace. The books published reflect the views of their authors and do not represent the official position of the Maryknoll Society. To learn more about Maryknoll and Orbis Books, please visit our website at www.maryknoll.org.

"The secret of life lies in laughter and humility": from chapter 9 of *Heretics;* as it appears in CW3, 107. "There was some one thing that was too great for God to show us when He walked upon our earth, and I have sometimes fancied that it was His mirth": from chapter 9 of *Orthodoxy;* as it appears in CW1, 366.

Library of Congress Cataloging-in-Publication Data

Chesterton, G. K. (Gilbert Keith), 1874–1936.
    [Selections. 2003]
    Essential writings / G.K. Chesterton ; selected with an introduction by William Griffin.
       p. cm. – (Modern spiritual masters series)
    ISBN 1-57075-495-0 (pbk.)
    1. Spiritual life – Literary collections. 2. Spiritual life. I. Griffin, William, 1935- II. Title. III. Series.
PR4453.C4A6 2003
828'.91209 – dc21

                   2003009799

Contents

Sources

AC   Ada Chesterton. *The Chestertons*. London: Chapman & Hall, 1905.

AG   Alec Guinness. *Blessings in Disguise*. New York: Alfred A. Knopf, 1986.

AH   Archibald Henderson. *George Bernard Shaw: Man of the Century*. New York: Appleton-Century-Crofts, 1956.

ANW   A. N. Wilson. *Hilaire Belloc*. New York: Atheneum, 1984.

ASD   Alzina Stone Dale. *The Outline of Sanity: A Life of G. K. Chesterton*. Grand Rapids, Mich.: William B. Eerdmans, 1982.

CW   *G. K. Chesterton: Collected Works*. San Francisco: Ignatius Press, 1986–.

CW1   Volume 1: *Heretics; Orthodoxy; The Blatchford Controversies*. With Introduction and Notes by David Dooley. 1986.

CW2   Volume 2: *St. Francis of Assisi; The Everlasting Man; St. Thomas Aquinas*. Introductions by George William Rutler, Larry Azar, and Raymond Dennehy. 1986.

CW3   Volume 3: *Where All Roads Lead; The Catholic Church and Conversion; Why I Am a Catholic; The Thing — Why I Am a Catholic; The Well and the Shallows; The Way of the Cross*. 1990.

CW4   Volume 4: *What's Wrong with the World; The Superstition of Divorce; Eugenics and Other Evils; Divorce versus Democracy; Social Reform versus Birth Control*. Introduction by James V. Schall, S.J. 1987.

CW11   Volume 11: *Plays; Chesterton on Shaw*. Ed. Dennis J. Conlon. 1989.

CW16   Volume 16: *The Autobiography*. Introduction by Randall
        Paine. 1988.

CW21   Volume 21: *What I Saw in America; The Resurrection of
        Rome; Sidelights*. Introduction by Robert Royal. 1990.

CW27   Volume 27: *The Illustrated London News: 1905–1907*. Ed.
        Lawrence J. Clipper. 1986.

DA3   Dale Ahlquist. Miscellaneous comments on the American
        Chesterton Society website: *http://www.chesterton.org*.

EB   "G. K. Chesterton," *Encyclopædia Britannica*. 15th ed.
        Chicago: Encyclopædia Britannica, Inc., 1980, Micropædia,
        2:815.

FB   *The Father Brown Omnibus*. New and rev. ed. New York:
        Dodd, Mead & Company, 1951.

GW1   Garry Wills. *Chesterton*. Rev. ed. New York: Doubleday Image,
        2001, 1975, 1961.

GW2   ———. *Why I Am a Catholic*. Boston: Houghton Mifflin,
        2002.

HB   Hilaire Belloc. *On the Place of Gilbert Chesterton
        in English Letters*. London: Sheed & Ward, 1940;
        as it appears on the G. K. Chesterton website:
        http://www.dur.ac.uk/martin.ward/gkc.

HL   Hugh Lunn. "Interview with G. K. Chesterton," *Hearth and
        Home*, October 17, 1912; as it appears on the G. K. Chesterton
        website: *http://www.dur.ac.uk/martin.ward/gkc*.

JC   Judy Cannato. "Paradox Road," *Weavings* (November–
        December 2001): 39–45.

JCT   John C. Tibbetts. "The Case of the Forgotten Detectives:
        The Unknown Crime Fiction of G. K. Chesterton"; *The
        Armchair Detective* 28, no. 4 (Fall 1995): 388–93; as
        it appears on the American Chesterton Society website:
        http://www.chesterton.org.

JP   Joseph Pearce. *Wisdom and Innocence: A Life of G. K.
        Chesterton*. San Francisco: Ignatius Press, 1996.

JS James Sauer. "Chesterton Reformed: A Protestant Interpretation"; as it appears on the "G. K. Chesterton," website: *http://www.dur.ac.uk/martin.ward/gkc.*

MFF Michael Ffinch. *G. K. Chesterton: A Biography.* San Francisco: HarperSanFrancisco, 1986.

MW Maisie Ward. *Gilbert Keith Chesterton.* New York: Sheed & Ward, 1943.

OCEL5 "G. K. Chesterton." *Oxford Companion to English Literature.* 5th ed. Ed. Margaret Drabble. New York: Oxford University Press, 1985, 190–91.

PY Philip Yancey. "G. K. Chesterton: Relics Along the Seashore." In *Soul Survivor: How My Faith Survived the Church.* New York: Doubleday, 2001, 43–60.

Introduction

Introducing Humor into the Divine

"We must be grateful indeed to a speaker who can occasionally introduce Humor into the Divine."

That could very well have been the first line of a memorial to Gilbert Keith Chesterton, happily remembered as the great Christian writer who flourished in the first third of the last century.

But no, the flattery came from a rather sour review in the *Gownsman*, one of Cambridge University's student rags, reporting on a two-hour address to the "Heretics," one of the university's student societies, on November 18, 1911.

Chesterton was an entirely appropriate speaker for that rag-tag group. Some years earlier he'd ragged heretics in general and modern heretics in particular in his newspaper columns, which subsequently appeared in book form entitled, appropriately enough, *Heretics* (1905).

That night at the ancient university on the River Cam, when he praised "paganity," he got a standing ovation, but then he led the students on a merry rhetorical chase, showing that they weren't the noble and observant pagans of old who had a stern, almost unforgiving moral sense, but rather a bunch of misguided youth who'd invited an irreverent, if irrelevant, adult to attack just about everything they stood for. Needless to say, a good time was had by all! (MFF, 201–2).

Who Was He?

Who was "this tomboy among dictionaries, this philosophical Peter Pan, this humorous Dr. Johnson, this kindly and gallant cherub, this profound student and wise master"? (quoted in PY, 51).

Who was this "world-famous literary genius, world-renowned essayist, dramatist, romanticist, poet, epigrammist, wit, phrase-maker, philosopher whose ideas attract, fascinate, impress — make people think"? (quoted in MFF, 5).

Who was this "visitor out of some fairy tale... legend in the flesh... survival of the childhood of the world"? Who was this "wayfarer from the ages, stopping at the inn of life, warming himself at the fire and making the rafters ring with his jolly laughter"? (quoted in JP, 137).

Well, Chesterton was all of these during his lifetime, and more. Often he was Pagliacci but more often Punchinello. Sometimes a Braggart Soldier, but more often a Swaggart Apologist. On occasion he was a Colossus, an Elgin Marble, even a Falstaff ("a goodly portly man, i' faith, and a corpulent" [I Henry IV, 2]). Certainly he was each and every character in each and every fairy tale he ever read — and that would include Cinderella and the Ugly Sisters.

But today as we look back, he was just a bloke like the rest of us, only a little more so. That's to say, for the Christian intellectuals and would-be apologists among us who, from time to time, enjoy mixing it up with the atheists and agnostics of our own age, Chesterton has a great deal to offer.

Who Were They?

For generations the Chestertons were descended from men of property. Alas, not inherited property of their own; just the inherited property of others. Chesterton & Sons were estate agents successfully handling transfers of property from the middle of the nineteenth century down to the present day. That occupation awaited Gilbert and his younger brother Cecil. Alas, only Cecil seemed to have had some aptitude for it, and hence he was sent to learn surveying, estate evaluation, and auctioneering.

Gilbert, on the other hand, responded right off, at the earliest age, to his father's vast love for English literature. From the family library he read, and he talked about his reading with Mr. Ed, as his father was called; and he memorized and recited what he memorized; and he debated what he'd read. His mother, Marie Louise, fostered the debates between father, brother, friendly neighbors, even casual visitors. House rules: don't raise your voice, and don't interrupt another.

After St. Paul's School for boys, Gilbert was sent to University College, London, where he encountered the classics and the other liberal arts, including the fine arts, which were found in the Slade, a burgeoning department of the college named after its benefactor. Among his professors were two scholars of note, A. E. Housman for Greek and Latin literature, and W. P. Ker for English literature.

From the professorial point of view, Chesterton appeared an indifferent student when he appeared at all and, as if to prove their suspicion, he dropped out after a couple of years. But, as not infrequently happens with talented students, such education as he'd gotten from his professors, and indeed given himself, left him at the age of twenty-two a formidably educated young man. There could only be one job for the likes of him, and that had to be in publishing. For the next five years he worked as manuscript reader and general factotum at two small houses.

On June 28, 1901, Chesterton married Frances Blogg in an Anglo-Catholic ceremony. They honeymooned on the Norfolk Broads for six days, creating a union that Augustine of Hippo would describe as an exchange of charities as well as chastities. It also created, as noted by biographer Joseph Pearce, a poem entitled "Creation Day." Its last lines surely describe the lovely coming together of two disparate souls. "The world is many and is mad, / But we are sane and we are one" (as cited in JP, 41).

Needless to say, each required a good deal of babying from the other. They adored the children of others; Gilbert especially, with his triumphant toy theater productions on all sorts of occasions. And in time there was even a child of their own. Dorothy Collins was the umpteenth secretary they'd hired, the first one with any sort of professional experience behind her; that was in 1926. She became their daughter in virtually every way, working through the deaths of her unofficially adopted parents and becoming executrix of their estates.

How He Behaved

While he'd been wooing Frances, Gilbert told his brother Cecil that she'd accepted him as he was; that was to say, as a rumpled stiltskin (he was towery, she was tiny). But when she hinted in a letter that his tidiness could be improved, he replied, "I am clean. I am wearing a frock coat, which from a superficial survey seems to have no end of buttons" (MFF, 59). When she suggested, again in a letter, that he might need a haircut, he replied that his hair seemed "pretty happy" and that perhaps it was "he, not his hair," that wanted cutting (MFF, 76).

Yes, these were the cutesy sort of answers a curly-headed boy gave Nursey every time she suggested he should shape up. Yes, this was the little boy who thought he could talk his way out of every naughtiness. And yes, this was the same nursery in which he'd read all the Fairy Tales of the West, and in them gleaned all the Wisdom of the West, and at the same time acquired a lifetime of bad habits. Did he have to take a bath? Did he have to clean his teeth? Did he have to straighten his hair? Did he have to pick up his things? Did he have to brush his clothes? Did he have to arrive on time? Yes, "Chesterton believed in prolonging childhood, and he was never sorry he was a backward child" (MFF, 17). And yes, the boy, now an adult, was indeed a rumpled stiltskin and intended to remain so! An elf like himself shouldn't have to do for himself. That's what the women in his life were for. And so they did do for him, and apparently without rancor.

How He Appeared

When Gilbert met Frances, it had been love at first sight. Relatives noticed that he was a scarecrow and she was underfed (MFF, 56). But after only a few years of immoderate drinking and nonstop smoking, his physical appearance changed dramatically. He became puffy and soon blimpy (MFF, 122 et seq.). Whenever he dined at his mother's house, according to Cecil's wife Ada, "the table groaned with salmon, veal cutlets, cream meringues... with lashings of burgundy and crème de menthe" (AC, 73; as quoted in MFF, 170–71). Once, the butler at the J. M. Barrie's rented estate, climbing the stairs to deliver Chesterton's freshly pressed evening attire, was overheard to remark, "His trousers — it reminds you of going down the Underground" (MFF, 130). "Had I a met a tram car," he once apologized to an audience who feared his lateness meant an accident, "it would have been a great and, if I may say so, an equal encounter" (MW, 368). On settling in the country near Beaconsfield, or so he confided to a friend, the locals thought that he appeared at a distance to be either the village idiot or a Harrod's delivery van (MFF, 177).

Living reproach to him was George Bernard Shaw, his very good friend and foe, who was taller than he and thin as a rail with a whiskery whispery beard. He was like, as Chesterton once put it, "Venus de Milo — all that there is of him is admirable" (MFF, 172).

Shaw returned the compliment, referring to Chesterton as "a large, abounding, gigantically cherubic person who is not only large in body and mind beyond all decency, but seems to be growing larger as you look at him" (MFF, 4).

Such a compliment, thought Chesterton, but there was something decidedly aggravating about Shaw. He was a notorious abstainer from all good things and English, and an abuser of all who weren't abstainers.

In this and so many other ways Shaw was countercultural, but in this and so few other ways Chesterton succumbed to his own culture; his hook, line, and sinker were meat, tobacco, and alcohol. In fact, as he'd often say in public, the consumption of these three commodities was a natural right of the happy and healthy Edwardian and Georgian male; not only in quality but also, apparently, in quantity. But he did all these substances to excess, and his appearance showed it more with each passing day. And there was an ultimate price to pay: he lived sixty-two years; Shaw, ninety-four.

To return to his appearance, Chesterton was the messiest-looking regular on Newspaper Row and indeed at home, but Frances had this idea. Why not mask her husband's spreading mass and expanding girth with something the other eccentrics had? Something recognizably his. Something the caricaturists could immortalize. After all, according to one of his biographers, Alzina Stone Dale, "Shaw had his red beard and jaeger suits; Yeats, his floppy velvet bows; and Bland, his monocle and spats" (ASD, 73). Frances finally came up with a Count of Monte Cristo opera cape, a slouch hat that made him look like "Falstaff in a brigand's costume," and a sword-stick cane (ASD, 73). But would it work?

"Fleet Street crowds have been used to the ways of great men since Dr. Johnson and Dean Swift trod the paving stones," wrote Constance Smedley on spotting Chesterton coming toward her one day.

"Chesterton is enveloped in an abstraction so mighty that it neutralizes the attention of the passerby. His huge figure, enveloped in its cloak and shaded by a slouch hat, rolls through the streets unheeding his fellow beings. His eyes stare before him in a troubled dream; his lips move, muttering, composing, arguing. He is an imposing figure; of immense proportions, almost balloon-like with a fine impetuous head which rises over the surrounding crowds; his hair is properly shaggy, his countenance open and frank, wearing indeed a curious childlike unconsciousness in spite of the thought intensity that clouds his brow."

Apparently, thought Frances on reading Smedley's comments in *T. P.'s Weekly*, her costume had done the trick (MFF, 174).

That was in 1910. The same again in 1914, but with a different hat.

"Walking down Fleet street some day you may meet a form whose vastness blots out the heavens. Great waves of hair surge from under the soft, wide-brimmed hat. A cloak that might be a legacy from Porthos floats about his colossal frame. He pauses in the midst of the pavement to read the book in his hand, and a cascade of laughter descending from the head notes to the middle voice gushes out on the listening air. He looks up, adjusts his pince-nez, observes that he is not in a cab, remembers that he ought to be in a cab, turns and hails a cab. The vehicle sinks down under the unusual burden and rolls heavily away. It carries Gilbert Keith Chesterton" (JP, 212–13).

Who else? asked Frances of herself on putting down her copy of A. G. Gardiner's *Prophets, Priests, and Kings* (1914).

So much for his disheveled appearance and erratic behavior.

When it came to thinking and imagining and writing, however, he cleaned up quite nicely.

How He Wrote

Chesterton wrote in a vague and personal way; that's to say, in a set of mental pictures rather than in a series of deductions stating his philosophy. "I will not call it my philosophy; for I did not make it," he wrote in *Orthodoxy*. "God and humanity made it; and it made me" (CW1, 211). He didn't propose to prove a thing. Rather he proposed to take as common ground between himself and an average reader "this desirability of an active and imaginative life, picturesque and full of a poetical curiosity," again from *Orthodoxy,* "a life such as western man at any rate always seems to have desired" (CW1, 212).

Each essay or chapter he wrote was the end product of what he called the *idling process,* which was most definitely not one of the fruits of the industrial revolution. What he meant by this may well be illustrated by the first sentence of "On Lying in Bed," a classic essay in *Tremendous Trifles* (1909).

"Lying in bed would be an altogether perfect and supreme experience if only one had a colored pencil long enough to draw on the ceiling." That's to say, he'd rather wait for inspiration to come than chase after it in the street.

Once he fixed upon an idea or image or emotion, he proceeded to write or dictate with all deliberate speed until he finished. For all of his haste, though, he's seemed to many to get too lost too often in his narrative. Or did he? Not really. No compass for him. He hadn't lost his point. It was just that he liked to dawdle. Hence, any ramble of his may have seemed that it was through a disorderly wood, but it was always filled with exotic plants and the most wildly successful growth.

As for his perennial point of view, he didn't like anything that wasn't old, no matter how decrepit. Yes, he was a praiser of time past as well as an appraiser of time present. Modernization, which was most times synonymous with "Americanization," was the villain; it always seemed to bring ugliness with it.

What He Wrote

"The subject of all Chesterton's writings is the unseen presence of God in the modern world," Dale Ahlquist, editor of the journal *Gilbert,* has noted. "Indeed, the two ideas we take from

Chesterton are that religion begins with the realization that the world is a magical place, and that politics begins with the realization that all human beings have a God-like dignity. Every human transaction, therefore, whether social or economic, is an opportunity either to dignify or to exploit our fellow man" (DA3).

As poet, columnist, biographer, social theorist and commentator, playwright, mystery writer, travel writer, religion writer, Chesterton bore this theory out.

Poet

"Yes" was the answer Chesterton shot forth when interviewer Hugh Lunn inquired whether minor poets were unfairly sneered at, "and as a minor poet I feel it deeply" (HL). His first book of poems, *Greybeards at Play,* four satirical poems illustrated by the poet himself, was published in 1900. "This little book," wrote his father in reviewing the work for the *Speaker,* "marks a stage in the development of a kind of literature which has grown up in the last century — that of nonsense" (MFF, 77).

W. H. Auden would later think that the four poems it contained were some of the best pure nonsense verse in the English language. More and serious poetry would come — including "The Wild Knight," "The Battle of Lepanto," "The Ballad of the White Horse," and "The Donkey," perhaps the most perfect of Chesterton's religious lyrics — culminating in 2000 with *Collected Poems* published by Ignatius Press.

Columnist

"Sending articles to hell" — that's how Chesterton described writing his columns and sending them off to the newspapers (MFF, 209). He made the round trip to and from the *Daily News, Illustrated London News,* and *New Witness — G.K. Weekly* perhaps thirty-five hundred, perhaps four thousand times in all. All the product of idling, the investigative engine he once conferred on one of his minor detectives, Basil Grant.

"[He] goes nowhere and knows everything. He is a retired English judge who became so disillusioned with English law that he 'suddenly went mad on the bench' and fled the profession to live a humble recluse in a Lambeth garret. Basil absorbs what he calls *atmospheres* and scorns a dependence on mere data" (JCT).

In his long and checkered career as a writer of all genres, Chesterton himself didn't develop a reputation as being a fact-chaser. "Facts, how facts obscure the truth!" exclaimed Basil. "I never could believe in that man — what's his name, in those capital stories? — Sherlock Holmes. Every detail points to something, certainly; but generally to the wrong thing" (JCT).

According to his wife Frances, "He considered himself nothing beyond a jolly journalist who wanted to paint the town red, and was always wanting more buckets of red paint" (quoted in MFF, 129).

Biographer

Biography as a genre was still aborning when Chesterton embarked on such biographical and literary studies as *Robert Browning* (1903), *Charles Dickens* (1906), *George Bernard Shaw* (1909), *William Blake* (1910), *William Cobbett* (1925), *Robert Louis Stevenson* (1927), and *Chaucer* (1932).

Apparently, they achieved some success in the popular marketplace. I would certainly have included in this anthology selections from his two highly praised religious biographies — *St. Francis of Assisi* and *St. Thomas Aquinas* — if, on reading them in 2002, I hadn't found them so dreadful.

An example from *St. Francis of Assisi*.

"Francis of Assisi was slight in figure with that sort of slightness which, combined with so much vivacity, gives the impression of smallness. He was probably taller than he looked; middle-sized, his biographers say; he was certainly very active and, considering what he went through, must have been tolerably tough" (CW2, 80–81).

This is a biographer in need of help.

Another example, this one from *St. Thomas Aquinas.*

"His bulk made it easy to regard him humorously as the sort of walking wine barrel, common in the comedies of many nations; he joked about it himself. It may be that he, and not some irritated partisan of the Augustinian or Arabian parties, was responsible for the sublime exaggeration that a crescent was cut out of the dinner table to allow him to sit down. It is quite certain that it was an exaggeration; and that his stature was more remarked than his stoutness; but, above all, that his head was quite powerful enough to dominate his body" (CW2, 496).

This is a biographer in need of serious help.

Both biographies, an extravagant but pathetic display of his writing talents.

Perhaps they're not biographies at all. Perhaps they're hagiographies with virtues that are hidden from me. Perhaps they're really prose poems suitable for pious meditation. Perhaps even they're really autobiographies of Chesterton himself, tarted up as Assisi and Aquinas and mouthing what he'd say if he were playing the part of Assisi or Aquinas on the stage. On this last score alone I'd gladly retrieve these two works from my dustbin.

Social Theorist and Commentator

C. S. Lewis, a literary and apologetic descendant of Chesterton's, once developed the theory that he could tuck Theology into a juvenile fictional narrative, and nobody'd be the wiser. Certainly not the critics, for they never noticed anything. But the children would notice it, but know it under some other name. In this matter *The Chronicles of Narnia* would certainly have to be considered a success.

But Chesterton had been doing the same thing some decades before. In such works as *Manalive, The Man Who Knew Too Much, Tales of the Long Bow, The Poet and the Lunatics, Four Faultless Felons,* he'd stuff the artichoke; that's to say, he'd turn

his mystery stories into "loosely-knit novels about agrarian reform, the nobility of the common man, and the romance of
medievalism," according to John C. Tibbetts. "The whimsical
tone too often is forced and labored, and much of the book
is marred by [his] tendency to inject agrarian Distributionist
polemic into the proceedings" (JCT).

Playwright

"What about that play?" wrote Shaw to Chesterton on March 1,
1908, encouraging him to drop the essays and columns and
reinvent himself as a playwright.

"I shall deliberately destroy your credit as an essayist, as a
journalist, as a critic, as a Liberal, as everything that offers your
laziness a refuge, until starvation and shame drive you to serious dramatic parturition. I shall repeat my public challenge
to you; vaunt my superiority; insult your corpulence; torture
Belloc; if necessary, call on you and steal your wife's affections
by intellectual and athletic displays until you contribute something to the British drama.... Nothing can save you now except
a rebirth as a dramatist. I have done my turn; and I now call on
you to take yours and do a man's work" (quoted in MW, 26).

Shaw knew what he was talking about. He'd already left
careers as novelist and drama critic behind him to become
a playwright with social activist expectations. In the sixteen
years preceding this letter to the talented young Chesterton,
he'd already written and produced nine plays, one of them the
humongous *Man and Superman* (1905), whose theme vexed
Chesterton so much.

On October 30, 1909, Shaw wrote to Chesterton again, but
this time he was more specific. "I will pay you £100 down
on your contracting to supply me within three months with a
mechanically possible, i.e., stageable, drama dealing with the
experiences of St. Augustine after revisiting England." As a
postscript, Shaw pointed out that a play wasn't a literary lark; it

was a piece written "for the good of all souls" (quoted in MW, 235–36).

On April 5, 1912, Shaw tried again, this time writing to Frances, asking her to join in his elaborate plot. On one pre-arranged Sunday he'd drop in on Beaconsfield. That would give him a chance to read his new play to her husband. It was "about Christian martyrs, and perfectly awful in parts." Again Shaw hoped this would stimulate Chesterton to hit the boards himself (quoted in MW, 240).

Well, Chesterton did write for the stage, but only after he was good and ready. *Magic*, a fantasy-comedy in three acts, was produced late in 1913. As Shaw expressed his philosophy in his plays, so Chesterton did in his. There was a God, and there were demons, and there was no getting around the fact that they battled over souls.

The play ran a hundred performances in London and was a hit in Germany as well. Wrote one reviewer in the *Dublin Review*, "The drama is built on that secrecy which was called Greek Irony. The audience must know the truth when the actors do not know it. It is a weakness in a play like *Magic* that the audience is not in on the central secret from the start" (quoted in ASD, 190). The insightful reviewer was Chesterton himself.

"Circumstances led to my seeing *Magic* performed several times," wrote Shaw in the *New Statesman* of May 13, 1916, "and I enjoyed it more and more every time.... It was delightful to find that the characters which seem so fantastic and even ragdolly (stage characters are usually waxdolly) in his romances became credible and solid behind the footlights, just the opposite of what his critics expected" (quoted in JP, 198).

Seven more plays followed, but not in rapid succession, and at least one of them had an obvious religious theme.

Mystery Writer

Chesterton liked to read mysteries, and so he came to like them, and even to write them. What was it that attracted him?

"The moral meaning of the crimes," according to commentator Dudley Barker, "is concerned with an attempt to recover the lost sense of the wonder and glamor of everyday life" (quoted in JCT). In a sense crime is an attraction only in postlapsarian life, and detectives, professional or amateur, are the clergy who minister to the criminals. Was Father Brown Chesterton's only detective? No, according to Tibbetts. "Less celebrated than the mild, dumpy little priest are other investigators whose cases are just as exotic and methods just as delightfully unconventional as his. To be sure, only a few are professional detectives or policemen; more significantly, most are what Chesterton cryptically calls *buoyant amateurs* — retired judges, civil servants, escaped lunatics, and accused felons" (JCT).

If there were a Rogue's Gallery of GKC's Tecs, it would include, in addition to the estimable Father Brown, such investigative gents as Rupert and Basil Grant, Major Brown, Colonel Crane, Owen Hood, Captain Hilary Pierce, Commander Blair, Mr. Pond, Cyrus Pym, Michael Moon, John Hume, Dr. Judson, Alan Nadoway, John Conrad, Gabriel Gale, Horne Fisher, Gabriel Syme, Inspector Traill, Paul Forain, Father Stephen, Adrian Hyde.

Travel Writer

"I have never managed to lose my old conviction that travel narrows the mind," wrote Chesterton as the opening sentence of *What I Saw in America* (1922). What he saw there may have narrowed his mind, but it opened his eyes. "America is the only nation in the world that is founded on creed. That creed is set forth with dogmatic and even theological lucidity in the Declaration of Independence; perhaps the only piece of practical politics that is also theoretical politics and also great literature" (CW21, 37, 41).

Other trips, other books: *The New Jerusalem* (1921). *The Resurrection of Rome* (1930).

Religion Writer

Chesterton loved debate, the thump and thwack of it. His own physique, if not his physical prowess, promised a good match to anyone who wanted to stand up to him.

"I think there are fewer people now alive who understand argument...," he noted in his *Aquinas*. "Anyhow, one of the real disadvantages of the great and glorious sport that is called *argument*, is its inordinate length.... Being himself resolved to argue, to argue honestly, to answer everybody, to deal with everything, he produced books enough to sink a ship or stock a library; though he died in comparatively early middle age. Probably he could not have done it at all if he had not been thinking even when he was not writing; but above all thinking *combatively*. This, in his case, certainly did not mean bitterly or spitefully or uncharitably, but it did mean *combatively*" (CW2, 499).

Heretics, Everlasting Man, and *Orthodoxy* should surely sit in the same pew. But if one were to usher in his autobiography and hagiographies and conversion stories, not to mention all of his little columns, then one would have a very crowded pew indeed.

How He Is Thought Of Today

"Chesterton's vigor, idiosyncrasies, optimism, puns, and paradoxes," noted the Fifth Edition of the *Oxford Companion to English Literature*, "celebrate the oddity of life and the diversity of people and places with a peculiar and at times exhilarating violence." The same entry concluded that "much of his vast output has proved ephemeral" (OCEL5, 191).

Well, yes, the once proud teacup was sprouting brown veins. But certainly Chesterton could find solace in being considered an ephemeron, especially if it meant that the Fifth Edition (1985) had to spend fifty-eight lines to say he was a flop after the Fourth Edition (1967) had spent only fourteen lines to say he was a hit.

No doubt novelist Margaret Drabble, editor of the Fifth, would take the Fifth in this regard. No doubt also that what she meant in that sweeping statement was that his religious writing had waned in popularity. But, paradoxically, it's his religious writing that's pulling the weight today and, amazingly, his appeal spans the Christian denominational spectrum.

What Christians Have Thought

"Chesterton himself said that the modern age is characterized by a sadness that calls for a new prophet," Philip Yancey, an evangelical author has written; "not like the prophets of old who reminded people that they were going to die, but someone who would remind them that they are not dead yet. . . . I know he did that for me. Whenever I feel my faith going dry again, I wander to a shelf and pick up a book by G. K. Chesterton. The adventure begins all over again" (PY, 59–60).

"Chesterton . . . is a wonderful, wise, witty, and pious man," James Sauer, Director of Library, Eastern College, has had to confess. "After reading his works, I never leave the page without feeling edified. Then what's the problem? . . . I am a Protestant; an American Evangelical Protestant; a Conservative, Capitalistic, Bible-thumping American Evangelical Protestant; I am also a Calvinist. We all have our crosses to bear. Anyone who is familiar with the writings of Chesterton will see the great irony in my situation" (JS).

What Catholics Have Thought

When it came time for Alec Guinness to write his memoir in the 1980s, he remembered a Chestertonian sentence that had stuck in his mind since his conversion twenty-five years before.

" 'The Church is the one thing that saves a man from the degrading servitude of being a child of his own time.' Just a little more effort, I hope, and I may deny myself that extra pat of butter, the third glass of wine, one lascivious thought, and achieve a moment when irascibility is controlled, one bitchy remark left unsaid; and, more positively, find a way to make some small generous gesture without forethought, and direct a genuine prayer of good will toward someone I dislike. It is a fairly pitiful ambition after a quarter of a century of genuflexion" (AG, 44). Guinness had thought it was from *Orthodoxy,* but it's really from *The Thing: Why I Am a Catholic.*

When Garry Wills wrote the introduction to the reissue of his study of Chesterton, published in 2001, originally published in 1961, he remembered an instance from his youth. "In 1952, when I was in a Jesuit seminary, I had succumbed to a nihilist mood that makes me see no God or goodness in the world. A shrewd mentor, Father Joseph Fisher, pointed out to me how closely Chesterton seemed to be addressing my condition in his student notebooks, while he fought off the solipsism that had brought him close to suicide" (GW1, XVI). Chesterton managed to work free of his nihilism, and Wills did too.

In his *Why I Am a Catholic* (2002) Wills told the story again. Later in the book he named some of the people who'd helped him come to a fuller understanding of the Apostles' Creed: "Saint Augustine, Cardinal Newman, and Gilbert Chesterton" (GW2, 297).

Becoming a Modern Spiritual Master

At first blush, Chesterton doesn't seem a likely candidate for the title "Modern Spiritual Master." But those who know him and his works well are certain that he *is* a modern master — it's just that they're hard put to point to half a dozen passages in which he specifically described Spirituality.

And yet, long before Pope Pius XI named him "Defender of the Catholic Faith" in 1936, Fr. John O'Connor had spotted him. In a letter dated February 1903, after enjoying his columns in the *Speaker* and the *Daily News,* he felt compelled to write to Chesterton: "I am a Catholic priest, and though I may not find you quite orthodox in details, I...wish to thank you very heartily, or shall I say, to thank God for having gifted you with the spirituality which alone makes literature immortal..." (quoted in MFF, 114).

At second blush, Chesterton speaks so compellingly of Orthodoxy, his primal insight, that one cannot help but believe that he was, and through his writings still is, a modern spiritual master.

"This is the thrilling romance of Orthodoxy. People have fallen into a foolish habit of speaking of Orthodoxy as something heavy, humdrum, and safe. There never was anything so perilous or so exciting as Orthodoxy. It was sanity, and to be sane is more dramatic than to be mad. It was the equilibrium of a man behind madly rushing horses, seeming to stoop this way and to sway that, yet in every attitude having the grace of statuary and the accuracy of arithmetic. The Church in its early days went fierce and fast with any warhorse; yet it is utterly unhistoric to say that she merely went mad along one idea, like a vulgar fanaticism. She swerved to left and right, so exactly as to avoid enormous obstacles. She left on one hand the huge bulk of Arianism, buttressed by all the worldly powers to make Christianity too worldly. The next instant she was swerving to avoid an orientalism, which would have made it too unworldly. The orthodox Church never took the tame course or accepted the conventions; the orthodox Church was never respectable. It would have been easier to have accepted the earthly power of the Arians. It would have been easy, in the Calvinistic seventeenth century, to fall into the bottomless pit of predestination. It is easy to be a madman: it is easy to be a heretic. It is always easy to let the age have its head; the difficult thing is to keep one's own. It is always easy to be a modernist, as it is easy to be a snob. To have fallen into any of those open traps of error and exaggeration which fashion after fashion and sect after sect set along the historic path of Christendom — that would indeed have been simple. It is always simple to fall; there are an infinity of angles at which one falls, only one at which one stands. To have fallen into any one of the fads from Gnosticism to Christian Science would indeed have been obvious and tame. But to have avoided them all has been one whirling adventure; and in my vision the heavenly chariot flies thundering through the ages, the dull heresies sprawling and prostrate, the wild truth reeling but erect" (VI, *Orthodoxy*; CWI, 305–6).

At third blush, Chesterton certainly came to understand the mechanics of conversion, the primal religious experience, having undergone it several times himself. He began life as Liberal Unitarian, progressed to Anglican, and ended up Roman Catholic. He moved easily from the one to the other. Indeed he felt entirely at home in a mysterious world in which religion, especially Christianity, more especially Roman Catholicism, was a major part of the explanation. That's not to say he was shy about the shortcomings of each, but he never bashed one, especially the one he'd just left, in public. Such a sense of spiritual indebtedness to and personal fondness for each of them would certainly seem to be the mark of the Holy Spirit and surely mark him as a modern spiritual master.

His own personal piety in whatever denomination apparently was fervent but unremarkable. Alas, none of the physical phenomena of mysticism, although he could have put any one of them to good, immediate use! Alas, no stigmata, although the ostentatious marks would've made a fine, flashy accompaniment to his blustery no-nonsense intellectual approach to Christianity. Alas, no apparitions to speak of, although his own fervid imagination continually produced images as holy as any saint's. Alas, no bilocations, which he could certainly have used to help meet the excessive obligations he put on his personal calendar. Alas, no levitations or teleportations, which a man of his bulk could only envy in the previous recipients of such gifts; all saints, yes, but with lean and hungry looks.

As for personal defect, in addition to the ones already mentioned, he did hate church bells; especially the ones telling him that if he was in earshot, he was already late. Fortunately, his wife, Frances, had an easy, regular piety; it was one of her endearing traits; and over the decades she managed, more often than not, to get her very large bundle to church on time.

At fourth blush, this Modern Anthologist who's labored to uncover passages indicating modern spiritual mastery in Chesterton's works found himself belabored by his Editor at Orbis, a young learned gentleman to be sure, to prove that they did indeed contain Spirituality. This Anthologist then had to resort to some unlikely tools to uncover Chesterton's spiritual and literary DNA.

Developing Levels of Meaning

In the first centuries of the Christian Era, after the Scriptures had been gathered and canonized, the Greek and Roman Fathers — Dionysius the Areopagite, Gregory of Nazianzus, Andrew of Caesarea chief among them — came to realize that they were interpreting the Scriptures on at least four levels. Hence, this mnemonic epigram.

> *Littera gesta docet; quid credas, allegoria;*
> *Moralis quid agas; quo tendas, anagogia.*

> Literally, it's what's been done.
> Allegorically, it's what you believe.
> Morally, it's what you'll do.
> Anagogically, it's where you're headed.

Take the word *Jerusalem*, please.

Literally or historically, it's the Holy City.
Allegorically or metaphorically, it's the Church Militant.
Tropologically or morally, it's the Just Soul.
Anagogically or mystically, it's the Church Triumphant.

Without belaboring the pros and cons of multilevel interpretation, I think it safe to say that Chestertonia, and indeed the works of all other authors, may also be interpreted in multiple, but not necessarily the same, ways.

In Chesterton's case I've read his work not only on the primary level — that's to say, the literal level, although the primary level on occasion is figurative or allegorical or metaphorical — but also on such secondary levels as to reveal his Paradoxy, Hilarity, and Humility. These are three, but certainly not all, of the hallmarks of his writing. And these are the three highlights of this study of his spirituality. To these I'd add Scripture; sometimes, to illumine a dark Chestertonian passage quick as a firefly, all it takes is a scriptural quotation.

Why There Should Be Notes

"Chesterton never used footnotes, and he would be surprised and amused that we are propping up some of his pages with these little annotations." That's what the general editors of Ignatius Press's *G. K. Chesterton: Collected Works* noted in "A Note on the Notes." Their norm: "only for references clearly crucial to the context and of sufficient obscurity to send the well-educated reader to the encyclopedia" (cw3, 13).

Well, I'm one of those knowledgeable readers, and I've had to look up hundreds more items than Ignatius Press; and the encyclopedia was the source of less than half. Clearly, one of us has made a serious miscalculation.

Preferring to err in favor of excess, I've put headnotes before the selections and endnotes after the selections.

Headnotes

Each of the selections in this Anthology is prefaced by four brief notes; each an optic through which to view the spirituality. Paradoxy, Hilarity, Humility, and Scripture. Perhaps a few words about each is in order.

Paradoxy

As surely as Orthodoxy runs through Chesterton's work, so does Paradoxy. It's a parallel rail, so to speak, on which he freighted his immense intellectual and imaginative output. Logic on one rail running in one direction. Imagination on the other rail, running in the opposite direction.

Yes, Chesterton was a logical man, but his logic wasn't always linear. In fact, more often than not it was curvilinear, paradoxical, roundabout, circumnavigative, often coming to conclusions without making the necessary connectives, but somehow managing to produce some stunning effects. For example. . . .

Without Hilarity Humility can be a very mean virtue. (Paradox mine.)

Hilarity

With Hilarity Humility can be a very rich virtue. Another fine paradox. The primal spiritual virtue combined with the primal secular virtue. A conjunction or juxtaposition of incongruities. Oddly enough, this too is a definition of comedy, whose noblest effect is Hilarity.

I could praise Hilarity for paragraphs but, suffice it to say, I've elevated Hilarity, if only for this small Anthology, to one of the moral virtues, together with Prudence, Justice, Temperance, and Fortitude; and to one of the theological virtues, along with Faith, Hope, and Charity. "Let nothing you dismay!"

But can Hilarity seriously be ranked as a religious virtue and can paradox really be ranked as a literary virtue?

"[Chesterton's] essays," noted an anonymous editor at the *Encyclopædia Britannica*, "developed his pawky, paradoxical irreverence to its ultimate point of real seriousness." The point is well made, but there's a better point to make. "Pawky, Paradoxical Irreverence" is its own justification, and needs no other relational dependence on a supposedly higher principle; that's to say, Real Seriousness.

Why? Because we live in the golden age of comedy, at least in the western world. People who dislike the dramatic arts may not think it, but it's so. More practitioners, more projects, more laughter. Most of it is disreputable and despicable, of course, and vulgar, in terrible taste, I'll be the first to admit. But when comedy's on target, which it surely is when people laugh, we recognize ourselves in it and laugh ourselves silly at it. That's been comedy's checkered history. Like cotton it's the fabric of our lives, right next to, if not already under, our skin.

This is not to say that Chesterton was a baggy-pants, music hall apologist. It's just to say that he was one of the funniest people of his own generation. Most of the others — Shaw, Belloc, Baring, Wells, funny fellows all — were his personal friends if not his amiable foes. They too are part of the history of comedy.

"Remember," Owen Barfield told me when he learned I was writing a biography of his longtime friend C. S. Lewis, "remember, he was a very funny man!" No one needed to remind me of that about Chesterton. And the selections that follow all contain sure and certain proofs of that.

Can Chesterton laugh at his own jokes?

"If a man may not laugh at his own jokes, at whose jokes may he laugh?" replies Chesterton in his own behalf, "May not an architect laugh in his own cathedral?" (MFF, 3).

Chesterton could give it, but could he take it?

When it came to debate, he rained down upon his opponent all the thrusts and ripostes he could, the more in a given amount of time, the better. But what happened when the adversary responded in kind? I have the following testimony from one bruised and battered adversary.

"To hear Chesterton's howl of joy...to see him double himself up in an agony of laughter at my personal insults, to watch the effect of sportsmanship on a shocked audience won to mirth by his intense and pea-hen-like quarks of joy was a sight and sound for the gods....It was monstrous, gigantic, amazing, deadly, delicious" (quoted in PY, 56–57).

No doubt there are readers of this Anthology who think they need no help from headnotes or endnotes in understanding Chesterton's comedy, and perhaps they're right. But these are precisely the people, I can almost hear Chesterton respond in my behalf, who are in most need of help. Although almost all of his jokes and japes retain their perfect timing, not all of them have retained their timeliness. Such notes as there are are meant to overcome this barrier. *Caveat cacchinans!* (Laugher, beware!)

To experience Chesterton's comic touch more directly, you may want to pick one of the selections that tickled your fancy first time round and spend half an hour with it, reading it slowly as one would do in *lectio divina,* savoring every witticism. Then read it out loud as Chesterton might have delivered it; that would be *lectio comica.*

Humility

In spirituality the virtue of Humility matters the most; yet in the manner of explanation it requires the least. Suffice it to say, Love has a number of spiritual honorifics. It is the great commandment, the third theological virtue. But on the hoof Love mummers as Humility. Thought to be, and indeed taught to be, a somewhat passive virtue, it is really, paradoxically, quite an aggressive virtue. Indeed as used in this Anthology it is meant to be a collective noun for all the virtues and commandments.

Scripture

Chesterton doesn't cite all that many scriptural verses directly in his works. But every now and then there's a passage or a newspaper column or a book chapter that looks like, walks like, talks like an *exemplum;* a staple in preaching since medieval times, meaning a parable, fable, or proverb in a sermon or discourse meant to illustrate, put a picture to, the exceedingly abstract considerations preachers always urge upon their congregations.

What Bible did Chesterton use? No doubt the King James Version when he was Church of England. When he became Church of Rome, perhaps he dipped into the Latin Vulgate of Jerome, Englished by no less a talented bunch of translators than the KJV enjoyed, but with somewhat less literary success, into the Douay (Old Testament)-Rheims (New Testament) Version.

For this Anthology I thought it appropriate to cite the Latin Vulgate and render the cited passages into English the way Chesterton might have; that's to say, in his own brand of brassy English. Only in this way will his Hilarity and Humility flower.

Please note that book titles as well as chapter and verse numbers in the Latin Vulgate don't always correspond to those in, for example, the New Revised Standard Version; where there's disparity, citations are given to both versions.

How Paradox Works

Perhaps a few more words of description need to be said to help us understand how Chesterton wielded paradox.

How does paradox work?

At its source, paradox is a comparison with or to someone or something. Often it's a Parallelism. Metaphor and Simile may also be involved.

It begins with a statement, general or particular, and it closes with another such statement. The closing may be an enrichment of the opening or, more often, the contradictory, contrary, or opposite of the opening. But with a twist, perhaps of lemon, perhaps of lime. But there's always a surprise.

Rhetorically, it's a manipulative trope. Yes, there can be some persuasion, some legerdemain with the logic.

Responsively, it makes one party happy; another party sad.

Is paradox an argument?

Some think it an argument, or would like to think it an argument. But at the moment one encounters a paradox, the reader or listener doesn't really know if the opening and closing statements are true or false or somewhere in between. The temptation is to think that, if the one generating the paradox has been truthful in the past, then the newly created paradox must also be true. Which would mean, among other things, that Chesterton never generated a false paradox in his life. And yet a lorry of them sound good but on closer examination just aren't sound argument. But that doesn't mean they all don't entertain.

Does paradox make a good argument?

Not really. It isn't much like a syllogism, a formula of argument with three terms: an opener and a closer with a middle term that does all that greasy, grimy work of argumentation.

If anything, it's rather more like an enthymeme; it has only two terms, a premise and a conclusion; but between the two there's more than enough wiggle room to generate a lot of logical mischief.

Is paradox reversible?

Yes, it's a lot like London Fog apparel in that much of it is reversible. Hence, a writer or speaker who brains his opponent with a paradox may find, within seconds, that very same paradox, with the terms reversed, heading right for his own skull!

All of which is to say, as you read the myriad of paradoxes in this anthology, that it's safer to consider each paradox as an entertainment rather than an argument until one's had the chance to give the terms of the paradox a thorough examination.

So much for how a paradox works.

How may paradox be defined?

In a number of ways. According to Belloc, in any audience he ever addressed there were at least two definitions fighting for supremacy. The Under-educated didn't know a paradox from a parasol but certainly enjoyed that paradoxical sparkle; for them paradox was just "nonsense through contradiction." The Over-educated among them, however, knew a paradox when they read or heard one; for them it was "illumination through an unexpected juxtaposition" (HB).

Is an unreliable trope like paradox really appropriate to describe the spiritual life?

Well, yes. According to Judy Cannato, spiritual director of a Wellness Center in Cleveland, "Paradox is the language of mature spiritual life."

Did Jesus use paradox?

"Jesus liked paradox and used the form to teach the mysteries of faith: a seed must die in order to live; the first will be last; you must lose your life to find it. The apostle Paul was familiar with paradox, too, evident when he declared that power is made perfect in weakness."

What about the contradictions contained in a paradox?

They "command our attention, and if we contemplate the incongruities that are the substance of the paradox, we can be drawn beyond our customary way of thinking" (JC, 40).

By the way, periods of prayer and reflection are ideal times during which to weigh the veracity of the opening and closing statements of spiritual paradox.

Selections

The selections chosen for this Anthology have as their purpose to reveal the rough-tough tools, habits, virtues, of a Christian intellectual, hopefully as they are found in the human heart, mind, and soul. They're found also in the word-to-word, trope-to-trope combat that is the debate, the classical confrontation of the Christian with the age he or she lives in.

This and the other volumes in the Masters of Modern Spirituality Series claim to present the "essential writings." Well, so humongous an output as Chesterton's means that a hundred anthologies of this size could be done without the duplication of a single selection. But in this slender volume, this pathetic sampling, I do contend that there's more than enough DNA to divine his spirituality.

The texts in this Anthology have been gathered from hither and yon (England and America). Covering a publishing period of a hundred years, they contain an amazing variety of decisions about everything relating to the fine (and perhaps deadly) art of copyediting, the blue pencil in inexperienced hands having become something of a stiletto.

For this collection only I have regularized capitalization and modernized spelling, punctuation, and paragraphing according to current American standards.

With regard to paragraphing, well, to put it mildly, Chestertonian paragraphs are generally obese, great gobs of continuous prose on a variety of topics, and expressing a variety of opinions, separated only occasionally by paragraph indents.

Consider then, if you will, Chesterton himself at the dinner table, a starched linen napkin tucked into his collar and draping his expansive front, addressing the mound of food on his plate. Consider also that each morsel, each titbit, each scrap on that plate, is a different thought or a different topic.

Fork in left hand, knife in right hand, GKC's blade crimps and cramps and crumps as many orts onto, and sometimes through, the hump-backed tines of his fork, creating a Fine Mash, prior to the Great Elevation, which is preparatory to the Grand Swallow.

That's how Chesterton wrote each and every paragraph. He could swallow it, and supposedly his contemporary readers could swallow it. We moderns can too, but we don't have to and indeed don't want to. Modern paragraphing is the only appropriate physick. And so I've done, without any diminution of meaning and, in some cases, with some clarification of meaning. Which is another way of saying, his diction remains intact.

Second Time Around

A little mischief, a little mysticism — yes, reading Chesterton the second time round was better than the first.

Noses abounded; cardboard noses for Guy Fawkes Day; a lady whose nose was the size of the Eiffel Tower; a gentleman who donated his nose to an elephant on the condition that it never be returned.

Umbrellas ubiquitous; Shaw threatening to smite Chesterton and Belloc over the head with his wife's umbrella; Chesterton's turning Fr. John O'Connor and his smartly rolled brolly into Father Brown and his battered bumbershoot.

Elves always underfoot, the small mischievous kind, not the handsome Tolkeinian hulks with pointy ears; Chesterton himself, who had many fine elvish qualities, would've made such a fine Tolkeinian elf!

Griffins, I was delighted to discover, seem to be Chesterton's mythical creature of choice, especially imagined as being of enormous size and strength such as himself; in his *Autobiography* he had occasion to refer to himself as a "Fabulous Griffin" (CW16, 173). Not that there's anything wrong with that.

Final Paradox

"Yes," said Father Brown in the opening line of "The Oracle of the Dog" (*The Incredulity of Father Brown*, 1915); "I always like a *dog* so long as he isn't spelled backward" (FB, 481).

Fortunately for us, paradoxically for Chesterton, he spelled it both ways.

1

HABITS OF HEART

DISCOVERING ENGLAND

Paradoxy: Yachtsman circumnavigating the globe in search of truth, only to find it waiting for him back home. *Hilarity:* "What could be more delightful than to have in the same few minutes all the fascinating terrors of going abroad combined with all the humane security of coming home again?" *Humility:* the one thing he hates most is the one thing he's accused of, being a smart aleck. *Scripture:* "On your way to the Master Mariner? I'm the chart, the course, the voyage. Who is He? He and I are one and the same" (John 14:6–7).

I have often had a fancy for writing a romance about an English yachtsman who slightly miscalculated his course and discovered England under the impression that it was a new island in the South Seas. I always find, however, that I am either too busy or too lazy to write this fine work, so I may as well give it away for the purposes of philosophical illustration.

There will probably be a general impression that the man who landed (armed to the teeth and talking by signs) to plant the British flag on that barbaric temple which turned out to be the Pavilion at Brighton, felt rather a fool.

I am not here concerned to deny that he looked a fool. But if you imagine that he felt a fool, or at any rate that the sense of folly was his sole or his dominant emotion, then you have not studied with sufficient delicacy the rich romantic nature of

41

the hero of this tale. His mistake was really a most enviable mistake; and he knew it, if he was the man I take him for.

What could be more delightful than to have in the same few minutes all the fascinating terrors of going abroad combined with all the humane security of coming home again? What could be better than to have all the fun of discovering South Africa without the disgusting necessity of landing there? What could be more glorious than to brace one's self up to discover New South Wales and then realize, with a gush of happy tears, that it was really old South Wales.

This at least seems to me the main problem for philosophers, and is in a manner the main problem of this book. How can we contrive to be at once astonished at the world and yet at home in it? How can this queer cosmic town, with its many-legged citizens, with its monstrous and ancient lamps, how can this world give us at once the fascination of a strange town and the comfort and honor of being our own town?

To show that a faith or a philosophy is true from every stand-point would be too big an undertaking even for a much bigger book than this; it is necessary to follow one path of argument; and this is the path that I here propose to follow.

I wish to set forth my faith as particularly answering this double spiritual need, the need for that mixture of the familiar and the unfamiliar which Christendom has rightly named *romance*. For the very word "romance" has in it the mystery and ancient meaning of Rome. Any one setting out to dispute anything ought always to begin by saying what he does not dispute. Beyond stating what he proposes to prove, he should always state what he does not propose to prove. The thing I do not propose to prove, the thing I propose to take as common ground between myself and any average reader, is this desirability of an active and imaginative life, picturesque and full of a poetical curiosity, a life such as western man at any rate always seems to have desired.

If a man says that extinction is better than existence or blank existence better than variety and adventure, then he is not one of the ordinary people to whom I am talking. If a man prefers nothing, I can give him nothing. But nearly all people I have ever met in this western society in which I live would agree to the general proposition that we need this life of practical romance; the combination of something that is strange with something that is secure. We need so to view the world as to combine an idea of wonder and an idea of welcome. We need to be happy in this wonderland without once being merely comfortable. It is *this* achievement of my creed that I shall chiefly pursue in these pages.

But I have a peculiar reason for mentioning the man in a yacht who discovered England. For I am that man in a yacht. I discovered England. I do not see how this book can avoid being egotistical; and I do not quite see (to tell the truth) how it can avoid being dull. Dullness will, however, free me from the charge which I most lament; the charge of being flippant. Mere light sophistry is the thing that I happen to despise most of all things, and it is perhaps a wholesome fact that this is the thing of which I am generally accused.

I know nothing so contemptible as a mere Paradox; a mere ingenious defense of the indefensible. If it were true (as has been said) that Mr. Bernard Shaw lived upon paradox, then he ought to be a mere common millionaire, for a man of his mental activity could invent a sophistry every six minutes. It is as easy as lying — because it is lying. The truth is, of course, that Mr. Shaw is cruelly hampered by the fact that he cannot tell any lie unless he thinks it is the truth. I find myself under the same intolerable bondage. I never in my life said anything merely because I thought it funny; though, of course, I have had ordinary human vainglory and may have thought it funny because I had said it.

It is one thing to describe an interview with a Gorgon or a Griffin, a creature who does not exist. It is another thing to

discover that the rhinoceros does exist and then take pleasure in
the fact that he looks as if he didn't. One searches for truth, but
it may be that one pursues instinctively the more extraordinary
truths. And I offer this book with the heartiest sentiments to
all the jolly people who hate what I write, and regard it (very
justly, for all I know) as a piece of poor clowning or a single
tiresome joke.

For if this book is a joke, it is a joke against me. I am the man
who with the utmost daring discovered what had been discovered
before. If there is an element of farce in what follows, the farce
is at my own expense; for this book explains how I fancied I was
the first to set foot in Brighton and then found I was the last.
It recounts my elephantine adventures in pursuit of the obvious.
No one can think my case more ludicrous than I think it myself;
no reader can accuse me here of trying to make a fool of him.

I am the fool of this story, and no rebel shall hurl me from
my throne. I freely confess all the idiotic ambitions of the end
of the nineteenth century. I did, like all other solemn little boys,
try to be in advance of the age. Like them I tried to be some ten
minutes in advance of the truth. And I found that I was eighteen
hundred years behind it. I did strain my voice with a painfully
juvenile exaggeration in uttering my truths. And I was punished
in the fittest and funniest way, for I have kept my truths. But I
have discovered, not that they were not truths, but simply that
they were not mine.

When I fancied that I stood alone, I was really in the ridicu-
lous position of being backed up by all Christendom. It may be,
Heaven forgive me, that I did try to be original; but I only succeeded in inventing all by myself an inferior copy of the existing
traditions of civilized religion. The man from the yacht thought
he was the first to find England; I thought I was the first to find
Europe. I did try to found a heresy of my own; and when I had
put the last touches to it, I discovered that it was *orthodoxy.*

It may be that somebody will be entertained by the account
of this happy fiasco. It might amuse a friend or an enemy to

read how I gradually learned from the truth of some stray legend or from the falsehood of some dominant philosophy, things that I might have learned from my catechism — if I had ever learned it. There may or may not be some entertainment in reading how I found at last in an anarchist club or a Babylonian temple what I might have found in the nearest parish church. If anyone is entertained by learning how the flowers of the field or the phrases in an omnibus, the accidents of politics or the pains of youth came together in a certain order to produce a certain conviction of Christian orthodoxy, he may possibly read this book. But there is in everything a reasonable division of labor. I have written the book, and nothing on earth would induce me to read it.

I add one purely pedantic note which comes, as a note naturally should, at the beginning of the book. These essays are concerned only to discuss the actual fact that the central Christian theology (sufficiently summarized in the Apostles' Creed) is the best root of energy and sound ethics. They are not intended to discuss the very fascinating but quite different question of what is the present seat of authority for the proclamation of that creed.

When the word "orthodoxy" is used here, it means the *Apostles' Creed,* as understood by everybody calling himself Christian until a very short time ago, and the general historic conduct of those who held such a creed. I have been forced by mere space to confine myself to what I have got from this creed; I do not touch the matter much disputed among modern Christians, of where we ourselves got it. This is not an ecclesiastical treatise but a sort of slovenly autobiography. . . .

English yachtsman: Evelyn Underhill, who plied the same spiritual waters, was in fact a Master Mariner whereas Chesterton couldn't sail a boat in his tub. This book: *Orthodoxy* (1908). *Pavilion at Brighton:* built by the Prince of Wales (later George IV) in 1784 as a summer residence and transformed by John Nash into an oriental palace. *Bernard Shaw:* drama critic, playwright, social reformer, general rhetorical

rascal; often debated GKC in print and in person. *Selections:* sub-
stitute in this book only for the GKC's original word "essays."
Source: Excerpt from "In Defense of Everything Else," chapter 1 /
introduction to *Orthodoxy,* 1908; as it appears in CW1, 211–15.

STUMBLING UPON STILTON

Paradoxy: a romantic ramble, real or imagined, through the country-
side searching for Englishness but finding only an unromantic town,
yet a spot romantic enough to inspire a crusty sonnet about a
crumbly cheese. *Hilarity:* a mock travel-writing style for this shaggy
tale; "Milton" made interchangeable with "Stilton"; a truly bad
poem, the sort that GKC and his literary pals thought truly good
verse in the nonsense manner of Edward Lear (1812–88). *Humility:*
a yearning, a *Sehnsucht,* for a once and future England; a Briga-
doon found, a Paradise lost; any one or all of these; or perhaps just
a hidden, vine-covered door to the Secret Garden where all good
spiritual lives begin. *Scripture:* "Explore, and you'll discover. Ask,
and you'll get directions. Knock, and watch the door swing open"
(Matthew 7:7).

I came along a lean, pale road south of the fens, and found
myself in a large, quiet, and seemingly forgotten village.

It was one of those places that instantly produce a frame of
mind which, it may be, one afterward decks out with unreal
details.

I daresay that grass did not really grow in the streets, but I
came away with a curious impression that it did.

I daresay the marketplace was not literally lonely and without sign of life, but it left the vague impression of being so.

The place was large and even loose in design, yet it had the
air of something hidden away and always overlooked.

It seemed shy, like a big yokel; the low roofs seemed to
be ducking behind the hedges and railings; and the chimneys
holding their breath.

I came into it in that dead hour of the afternoon which is
neither after lunch nor before tea, nor anything else even on a

half-holiday; and I had a fantastic feeling that I had strayed into a lost and extra hour that is not numbered in the twenty-four.

I entered an inn which stood openly in the marketplace yet was almost as private as a private house; those who talk of "public houses" as if they were all one problem would have been both puzzled and pleased with such a place.

In the front window a stout old lady in black with an elaborate cap sat doing a large piece of needlework; she had a kind of comfortable Puritanism about her, and might have been (perhaps she was) the original Mrs. Grundy.

A little more withdrawn into the parlor sat a tall, strong, and serious girl, with a face of beautiful honesty and a pair of scissors stuck in her belt, doing a small piece of needlework.

Two feet behind them sat a hulking laborer with a humorous face like wood painted scarlet, with a huge mug of mild beer which he had not touched, and probably would not touch for hours.

On the hearthrug there was an equally motionless cat; and on the table a copy of *Household Words*.

I was conscious of some atmosphere, still and yet bracing, that I had met somewhere in literature. There was poetry in it as well as piety; and yet it was not poetry after my particular taste. It was somehow at once solid and airy. Then I remembered that it was the atmosphere in some of Wordsworth's rural poems; which are full of genuine freshness and wonder, and yet are in some incurable way commonplace....

Certainly the whole of that town was like a cup of water given at morning.

After a few sentences exchanged at long intervals in the manner of rustic courtesy, I inquired casually what was the name of the town.

The old lady answered that its name was Stilton, and composedly continued her needlework.

But I had paused with my mug in air, and was gazing at her with a suddenly arrested concern.

"I suppose," I said, "that it has nothing to do with the cheese of that name."

"Oh, yes," she answered, with a staggering indifference, "they used to make it here."

I put down my mug with a gravity far greater than her own.

"But this place is a shrine!" I said. "Pilgrims should be pouring into it from wherever the English legend has endured alive. There ought to be a colossal statue in the marketplace of the man who invented Stilton cheese. There ought to be another colossal statue of the first cow who provided the foundations of it. There should be a burnished tablet let into the ground on the spot where some courageous man first ate Stilton cheese and survived. On the top of a neighboring hill (if there are any neighboring hills) there should be a huge model of a Stilton cheese, made of some rich green marble and engraven with some haughty motto. I suggest something like *Ver non semper viret; sed Stiltonia semper virescit.*"

The old lady said, "Yes, sir," and continued her domestic occupations.

After a strained and emotional silence, I said, "If I take a meal here tonight, can you give me any Stilton?"

"No, sir; I'm afraid we haven't got any Stilton," said the Immovable One, speaking as if it were something thousands of miles away.

"This is awful," I said, for it seemed to me a strange allegory of England as she is now. This little town that had lost its glory and forgotten, so to speak, the meaning of its own name.

And I thought it yet more symbolic because from all that old and full and virile life, the Great Cheese was gone; and only the beer remained. And even that will be stolen by the Liberals or adulterated by the Conservatives.

Politely disengaging myself, I made my way as quickly as possible to the nearest large, noisy, and nasty town in that neighborhood, where I sought out the nearest vulgar, tawdry, and avaricious restaurant. There (after trifling with beef, mutton, puddings, pies, and so on) I got a Stilton cheese. I was so much moved by my memories that I wrote a sonnet to the cheese.

Some critical friends have hinted to me that my sonnet is not strictly new; that it contains "echoes" (as they express it) of some other poem that they have read somewhere. Here, at least, are the lines I wrote:

SONNET TO A STILTON CHEESE

Stilton, thou shouldst be living at this hour
And so thou art. Nor losest grace thereby;
England has need of thee, and so have I —
She is a Fen. Far as the eye can scour,
League after grassy league from Lincoln tower
To Stilton in the fields, she is a Fen.
Yet this high cheese, by choice of fenland men,
Like a tall green volcano rose in power.
Plain living and long drinking are no more,
And pure religion reading *Household Words,*
And sturdy manhood sitting still all day
Shrink, like this cheese that crumbles to its core;
While my digestion, like the House of Lords,
The heaviest burdens on herself doth lay.

I confess I feel myself as if some literary influence, something that has haunted me, were present in this otherwise original poem; but it is hopeless to disentangle it now.

Half-holiday: afternoon off. *Original Mrs. Grundy:* character in *Speed the Plough,* a play by Thomas Morton (1764?–1838) produced in 1798; never seen but always referred to as the unforgiving She-Who-Must-Be-Obeyed of etiquette and propriety. *Household Words:* weekly periodical, started in 1850 by Dickens, including contributions by the notable writers of the day. *Stilton:* classic English blue cheese made from cow's milk; named for the village in Huntingdonshire where, according to tradition, it was first sold in the late eighteenth century at a stagecoach stop called the Bell Inn; apparently, it has been produced in surrounding shires, but never in its namesake village. *Ver...virescit:* "Spring's smell fades, but Stilton smells forever." *Sonnet:* parody, in more ways than one, of Wordsworth's sonnet "Milton! Thou shouldst be living at this hour." *Source:* Excerpt from "The Poet and the Cheese," second chapter in *A Miscellany of Men,* 1912.

FLYING THE FLAG ON THE TURRET

Paradoxy: The tick-tock of optimist-pessimist, right-left, good-bad, eyes-feet, dreary-happy, this world-other world, presence-absence, loyalty-admiration, sad-glad. *Hilarity:* One should love the world for its gladness. *Humility:* One should love the world for its sadness. *Scripture:* "You're from Here Below — I'm from Up Above. You're from This World — I'm not from This World. So what's that got to do with you? Only that you'll drown in your sins — yes, you'll drown in them if you don't come to believe that I'm the One" (John 8:23–24).

When I was a boy there were two curious men running about who were called the Optimist and the Pessimist. I constantly used the words myself, but I cheerfully confess that I never had any very special idea of what they meant. The only thing which might be considered evident was that they could not mean what they said, for the ordinary verbal explanation was that the Optimist thought this world as good as it could be while the Pessimist thought it as bad as it could be. Both these statements being obviously raving nonsense, one had to cast about for other explanations.

An Optimist could not mean a man who thought everything right and nothing wrong, for that is meaningless; it is like calling everything right and nothing left. Upon the whole, I came to the conclusion that the Optimist thought everything good except the Pessimist, and that the Pessimist thought everything bad, except himself.

It would be unfair to omit altogether from the list the mysterious but suggestive definition said to have been given by a little girl, "An Optimist is a man who looks after your eyes, and a

Pessimist is a man who looks after your feet." I am not sure that this is not the best definition of all.

There is even a sort of allegorical truth in it. For there might, perhaps, be a profitable distinction drawn between that more dreary thinker who thinks merely of our contact with the earth from moment to moment, and that happier thinker who considers rather our primary power of vision and of choice of road.

But this is a deep mistake in this alternative of the Optimist and the Pessimist. The assumption of it is that a man criticizes this world as if he were house-hunting, as if he were being shown over a new suite of apartments. If a man came to this world from some other world in full possession of his powers, he might discuss whether the advantage of midsummer woods made up for the disadvantage of mad dogs, just as a man looking for lodgings might balance the presence of a telephone against the absence of a sea view. But no man is in that position.

A man belongs to this world before he begins to ask if it is nice to belong to it. He has fought for the flag and often won heroic victories for the flag long before he has ever enlisted. To put shortly what seems the essential matter, he has a loyalty long before he has any admiration....

It . . . still seems to me that our attitude toward life can be better expressed in terms of a kind of military loyalty than in terms of criticism and approval. My acceptance of the universe is not Optimism, it is more like Patriotism. It is a matter of primary loyalty. The world is not a lodging house at Brighton, which we are to leave because it is miserable. It is the fortress of our family, with the flag flying on the turret, and the more miserable it is, the less we should leave it.

The point is not that this world is too sad to love or too glad not to love. The point is that when you do love a thing, its gladness is a reason for loving it, and its sadness a reason for loving it more. All optimistic thoughts about England and all pessimistic thoughts about her are alike reasons for the English

Patriot. Similarly, Optimism and Pessimism are alike arguments for the Cosmic Patriot.

> *Brighton:* seaside resort on the English Channel. *Source:* Excerpt from "The Flag of the World," chapter 5 of *Orthodoxy;* as it appears in cw1, 269–84.

SEEING THROUGH CHILDLIKE EYES

> *Paradoxy:* The more one becomes a child, the more one becomes an adult. *Hilarity:* Putting the right *entrée* into the right gentleman. *Humility:* The less one becomes an adult, the more one becomes a child. *Scripture:* "The crowd swelled, and the women surged, holding their babes in the air for the Holy Man to see and to touch. In the process the disciples got roughed up, and things got ugly. 'Now, now, now,' said Jesus to his closest friends; 'don't bunch your knickers! No need to drive them off. In fact, go round them up. Why? Well, it has something to do with the Kingdom of God. Listen closely. I'm going to say this only once. The Kingdom of God is like a playground. Toddlers know this. How come grownups don't? Think about it' " (Luke 18:15–17).

The only simplicity that matters is the Simplicity of the Heart.

If that be gone, it can be brought back by no turnips or cellular clothing, but only by tears and terror and the fires that are not quenched.

If that remain, it matters very little if a few Early Victorian armchairs remain along with it.

Let us put a complex *entrée* into a simple old gentleman; let us not put a simple *entrée* into a complex old gentleman.

So long as human society will leave my spiritual inside alone, I will allow it, with a comparative submission, to work its wild will with my physical interior. I will submit to cigars. I will meekly embrace a bottle of Burgundy. I will humble myself to a hansom cab. If only by this means I may preserve to myself the virginity of the spirit which enjoys with astonishment and fear.

I do not say that these are the only methods of preserving it. I incline to the belief that there are others. But I will have nothing to do with simplicity which lacks the fear, the astonishment, and the joy alike. I will have nothing to do with the devilish vision of a child who is too simple to like toys.

The child is indeed, in these and many other matters, the best guide. And in nothing is the child so righteously child-like, in nothing does he exhibit more accurately the sounder order of simplicity, than in the fact that he sees everything with a simple pleasure, even the complex things. The false type of naturalness harps always on the distinction between the natural and the artificial. The higher kind of naturalness ignores that distinction.

To the child the tree and the lamp post are as natural and as artificial as each other; or rather, neither of them are natural but both supernatural, for both are splendid and unexplained. The flower with which God crowns the one, and the flame with which Sam the lamplighter crowns the other, are equally of the gold of Fairy Tales.

In the middle of the wildest fields the most rustic child is, ten to one, playing at steam engines. And the only spiritual or philosophical objection to steam engines is not that men pay for them or work at them or make them very ugly or even that men are killed by them, but merely that men do not play at them.

The evil is that the childish poetry of clockwork does not remain.

The wrong is not that engines are too much admired, but that they are not admired enough.

The sin is not that engines are mechanical, but that men are mechanical.

Clockwork: mechanism, usually with wheels, that depends for its motion on being wound up with a spring; the mechanics of operation; what makes things go. *Source:* Excerpt from chapter 10, "On Scandals and Simplicity," *Heretics,* 1905; as it appears in CW1, 112–13.

2

HABITS OF MIND

PROPER FIRST PRINCIPLES

Paradoxy: "This balance of apparent contradictions...has been the whole buoyancy of the healthy man." *Hilarity:* Free Will as practiced by the Christian could very well ease relations with the housemaid. *Humility:* "Man can understand everything by the help of what he does not understand." *Scripture:* "The great command-ments? You should love the Lord your God. It'll take all your heart, soul, and mind, and while you're at it, put your shoulder into it as well. That's the first. The second's pretty much the same. You should love your neighbor if for no other reason than he's the mirror image of yourself. Any more? No, that's about it" (Mark 12:30–31).

What actually is the chief mark and element of insanity?...It is reason used without root, reason in the void. The man who begins to think without the proper first principles goes mad; he begins to think at the wrong end....If this be what drives men mad, what is it that keeps them sane?...It is possible in the...solely practical manner to give a general answer touching what in actual human history keeps men sane.

Mysticism keeps men sane. As long as you have mystery you have health; when you destroy mystery, you create morbidity.

The ordinary man has always been sane because the ordinary man has always been a Mystic. He has permitted the twilight. He has always had one foot in Earth and the other in Fairyland.

He has always left himself free to doubt his gods; but (unlike the Agnostic of today) free also to believe in them. He has always cared more for truth than for consistency. If he saw two truths that seemed to contradict each other, he would take the two truths and the contradiction along with them.

His spiritual sight is stereoscopic, like his physical sight: he sees two different pictures at once and yet sees all the better for that. Thus he has always believed that there was such a thing as fate, but such a thing as Free Will also. Thus he believed that children were indeed the Kingdom of Heaven, but nevertheless ought to be obedient to the Kingdom of Earth. He admired youth because it was young and age because it was not.

It is exactly this balance of apparent contradictions that has been the whole buoyancy of the healthy man.

The whole secret of Mysticism is this, that man can understand everything by the help of what he does not understand.

The Morbid Logician seeks to make everything lucid, and succeeds in making everything mysterious.

The Mystic allows one thing to be mysterious, and everything else becomes lucid.

The Determinist makes the theory of causation quite clear, and then finds that he cannot say "if you please" to the housemaid.

The Christian permits Free Will to remain a sacred mystery, but because of this his relations with the housemaid become of a sparkling and crystal clearness. He puts the seed of dogma in a central darkness, but it branches forth in all directions with abounding natural health.

As we have taken the circle as the symbol of reason and madness, we may very well take the cross as the symbol at once of mystery and of health. Buddhism is centripetal, but Christianity is centrifugal; it breaks out. For the circle is perfect and infinite in its nature, but it is fixed forever in its size; it can never be larger or smaller. But the cross, though it has at its heart a collision and a contradiction, can extend its four arms forever without altering its shape. Because it has a paradox in its center, it can grow without changing. The circle returns upon itself and is bound. The cross opens its arms to the four winds; it is a signpost for free travelers.

Symbols alone are of even a cloudy value in speaking of this deep matter; and another symbol from physical nature will express sufficiently well the real place of mysticism before mankind. The one created thing which we cannot look at is the one thing in the light of which we look at everything. Like the sun at noonday, Mysticism explains everything else by the blaze of its own victorious invisibility.

Detached Intellectualism is (in the exact sense of a popular phrase) all moonshine; for it is light without heat, and it is secondary light, reflected from a dead world. But the Greeks were right when they made Apollo the god both of imagination and of sanity, for he was both the patron of poetry and the patron of healing....

That transcendentalism by which all men live has primarily much the position of the sun in the sky. We are conscious of it as of a kind of splendid confusion; it is something both shining and shapeless, at once a blaze and a blur. But the circle of the moon is as clear and unmistakable, as recurrent and inevitable, as the circle of Euclid on a blackboard. For the moon is utterly reasonable; and the moon is the mother of lunatics and has given to them all her name.

Mysticism: In Chesterton's time the word had half a dozen meanings; by our time it has acquired half a dozen more. Then as now, it means at least "spirituality" as opposed to "materiality." *Mystery:* In general, a religious belief based on divine revelation; in particular, the central mystery of Christianity, the *Mysterium Tremendum,* the Godhead. *Euclid:* mathematician who flourished around 300 B.C.E., happily remembered for his treatise on geometry. *Source:* Excerpt from "The Maniac," chapter 2 of *Orthodoxy;* as it appears in CW1, 216–32.

PHILOSOPHIZING IN THE DARK

Paradoxy: the powers of light and darkness do battle. *Hilarity:* perhaps unintended Hilarity, but Chesterton's first move in discussing a modern problem was always to consult the medievals first. *Humility:* sometimes the dullest people provide the brightest answers. *Scripture:* "Don't fall for any of those fast-talking philosophies with the funny-sounding syllogisms. If you must have a philosopher, try Christ. Why not?" (Colossians 2:8).

Suppose that a great commotion arises in the street about something, let us say a lamp post, which many influential persons desire to pull down.

A Gray-clad Monk, who is the spirit of the Middle Ages, is approached upon the matter and begins to say, in the arid manner of the Schoolmen, "Let us first of all consider, my brethren, the value of Light. If Light be in itself good — "

At this point he is somewhat excusably knocked down.

All the people make a rush for the lamp post, the lamp post is down in ten minutes, and they go about congratulating each other on their unmedieval practicality.

But as things go on, they do not work out so easily.

Some people have pulled the lamp post down because they wanted the electric light; some because they wanted old iron; some because they wanted darkness because their deeds were evil.

Some thought it not enough of a lamp post, some too much; some acted because they wanted to smash municipal machinery; some because they wanted to smash something. And there is war in the night, no man knowing whom he strikes.

So, gradually and inevitably, today, tomorrow, or the next day, there comes back the conviction that the Monk was right after all, and that all depends on what is the philosophy of Light.

Only what we might have discussed under the gas lamp, we now must discuss in the dark.

Gray-clad Monk: Franciscans wore gray habits in the thirteenth and fourteenth centuries before switching to brown in the fifteenth; in the thirteenth the Grey Friars, as they've been continually called, created schools of Theology in such university towns as Paris and Oxford that set the standard in the rest of Europe. *Middle Ages:* from the fifth to the fifteenth centuries, that period in Europe between the fall of the Roman Empire and the rise of the New Humanism. Some historians, rather dimly lit themselves, have called it the Dark Ages; Chesterton here was referring to the High Middle Ages, the thirteenth and fourteenth centuries, where civilization burned very brightly indeed. *Schoolmen:* professors of, among other subjects, Philosophy and Theology in the medieval universities. *Source:* Excerpt from "Introductory Remarks," *Heretics,* 1905; as it appears in CW1, 46.

LOGIC AND LAWN TENNIS

Paradoxy: this isn't so much about the to-ings and fro-ings of Lawn Tennis as it is of Logic Tennis; that's to say, before one can logick contemporary Tennis, one must master classical Logic. *Hilarity:* this bit of Wimbledon whimsy contains faux biblical exegesis of the biblical needle (Mark 10:25), with angels at one end and camels at the other; medieval scholar-mystics proclaiming Tennis was made for Man, not the other way round; GKC's announcing the existence of "a certain Absolute and Divine Being whose name is Mr. Lawn Tennis" — surely a first in the history of natural theology. *Humility:* the mind has to bend to reason before it can influence the soul. *Scripture:* "You ought to be teachers by now, having mastered the basics about God. But no, you're still tots at the tit. You should be eating solid food by now, grown-up stuff for people who've learned how to discern good from evil" (Hebrews 5:12–14).

I read an article by the admirable Mr. Tilden, the great tennis player, who was debating what is wrong with English Tennis. "Nothing can save English Tennis," he said, except certain reforms of a fundamental sort, which he proceeded to explain. The English, it appears, have a weird and unnatural way of regarding tennis as a game, or thing to be enjoyed. He admitted that this has been part of a sort of amateur spirit in everything which is (as he very truly noted) also a part of the national character. But all this stands in the way of what he called saving English Tennis. He meant what some would call making it *perfect,* and others would call making it *professional.*

Now, I take that as a very typical passage, taken from the papers at random, and containing the views of a keen and acute person on a subject that he thoroughly understands. But what he does not understand is the thing which he supposes to be understood. He thoroughly knows his subject, and yet he does not know what he is talking about; because he does not know what he is taking for granted. He does not realize the relation of means and ends, or axioms and inferences, in his own philosophy. And nobody would probably be more surprised, and even legitimately indignant, than he if I were to say that the first principles of his philosophy appear to be as follows.

1. There is in the nature of things a certain Absolute and Divine Being whose name is Mr. Lawn Tennis.
2. All men exist for the good and glory of this Mr. Tennis and are bound to approximate to his perfections and fulfil his will.
3. To this higher duty they are bound to surrender their natural desire for enjoyment in this life.
4. They are bound to put this loyalty first; and to love it more passionately than patriotic tradition, the preservation of their own national type and national culture; not to mention even their national virtues.

That is the creed or scheme of doctrine that is here developed without being defined.

The only way for us to save the game of Lawn Tennis is to prevent it from being a game. The only way to save English Tennis is to prevent it from being English. It does not occur to such thinkers that some people may possibly like it because it is English and enjoy it because it is enjoyable. There is some abstract divine standard in the thing, to which it is everybody's duty to rise, at any sacrifice of pleasure or affection.

When Christians say this of the sacrifices made for Christ, it sounds rather a hard saying. But when Tennis Players say it about the sacrifices demanded by Tennis, it sounds quite ordinary and casual in the confusion of current thought and expression. And nobody notices that a sort of human sacrifice is being offered to a sort of new and nameless god.

In the good old days of Victorian Rationalism, it used to be the conventional habit to scoff at St. Thomas Aquinas and the Medieval Theologians; and especially to repeat perpetually a well-worn joke about the man who discussed how many angels could dance on the point of a needle. The Comfortable and Commercial Victorians, with their money and merchandise, might well have felt a sharper end of the same needle, even if it was the other end of it. It would have been good for their souls to have looked for that needle, not in the haystack of medieval Metaphysics, but in the neat needle case of their own favorite pocket Bible. It would have been better for them to meditate, not on how many angels could go on the point of a needle, but on how many camels could go through the eye of it. But there is another comment on this curious joke or catchword, which is more relevant to our purpose here.

If the Medieval Mystic ever did argue about angels standing on a needle, at least he did not argue as if the object of angels was to stand on a needle; as if God had created all the Angels and Archangels, all the Thrones, Virtues, Powers, and Principalities, solely in order that there might be something to clothe and decorate the unseemly nakedness of the point of a needle. But that is the way that modern rationalists reason. The Medieval Mystic would not even have said that a needle exists to be a standing-ground for angels. The Medieval Mystic would have been the first to say that a needle exists to make clothes for men.

For Medieval Mystics, in their dim transcendental way, were much interested in the real reasons for things and the distinction between the means and the end. They wanted to know what a thing was really for, and what was the dependence of one idea on another. And they might even have suggested, what so many journalists seem to forget, the paradoxical possibility that Tennis was made for Man and not Man for Tennis.

The Modernists were peculiarly unfortunate when they said that the modern world must not be expected to tolerate the old syllogistic methods of the Schoolmen. They were proposing to scrap the one medieval instrument which the modern world will most immediately require.

There would have been a far better case for saying that the revival of Gothic architecture has been sentimental and futile; that the Pre-Raphaelite movement in art was only an eccentric episode; that the fashionable use of the world "Guild" for every possible sort of social institution was affected and artificial; that the feudalism of Young England was very different from that of Old England.

But of this method of clean-cut deduction, with the definition of the postulates and the actual answering of the question, is something of which the whole of our newspaper-flattered society is in sharp and instant need; as the poisoned are in need of medicine.

I have here taken only one example which happened to catch my eye out of a hundred thousand that flash past every hour.

And as Tennis, like every other good game, has to be played with the head as well as the hand, I think it highly desirable that it should be occasionally discussed at least as intelligently as it is played.

William ("Big Bill") Tilden: dominant amateur tennis player in the 1920s, winning fifteen Davis Cup singles; won men's singles at Wimbledon in 1920, 1921, 1930. *Schoolmen:* professors of, among other subjects, Philosophy and Theology in medieval universities. *Pre-Raphaelite Brotherhood:* movement to infuse art with morality, flourishing in mid-nineteenth-century England; its members — most prominently, William Holman Hunt, John Everett Millais, Dante Gabriel Rossetti — contended that the degeneration of western art had begun in the Renaissance with Raphael. *Guild:* organization formed for the mutual aid and protection of its members, or for the furtherance of some common purpose; especially, a medieval association of craftsmen or merchants. *Source:* Excerpt from "Logic and Lawn Tennis," chapter 5 of *The Thing: Why I Am a Catholic,* 1929 as it appears in CW3, 165–68.

THE EXTRAORDINARY CABMAN

Paradoxy: after stoutly defending sanity and certainty, an apologist often feels kind of wobbly. *Hilarity:* a beery lunch among best friends turns into a metaphysical melee about certitude. *Humility:* even in the middle of his phantasmagoria, GKC realized that the Cabman was an honest man and "a member of a much more respectable profession." *Scripture:* "Why is it that when you need faith, you have so little of it?" (Matthew 6:30, 8:26, 14:31, 16:8).

From time to time I have introduced into this newspaper column the narration of incidents that have really occurred. I do not mean to insinuate that in this respect it stands alone among newspaper columns. I mean only that I have found that my meaning was better expressed by some practical parable out of daily life than by any other method. Therefore, I propose to narrate the incident of the Extraordinary Cabman, which occurred to me only three days ago and which, slight as it apparently is, aroused in me a moment of genuine emotion bordering upon despair.

On the day that I met the strange Cabman I had been lunching in a little restaurant in Soho in company with three or four of my best friends. My best friends are all either bottomless skeptics or quite uncontrollable believers, so our discussion at luncheon turned upon the most ultimate and terrible ideas. And the whole argument worked out ultimately to this, *that the question is whether a man can be certain of anything at all.*

I think he can be certain, for if (as I said to my friend, furiously brandishing an empty bottle) it is impossible intellectually to entertain certainty, what is this certainty which it is impossible to entertain? If I have never experienced such a thing as certainty, I cannot even say that a thing is not certain.

Similarly, if I have never experienced such a thing as green, I cannot even say that my nose is not green. It may be as green as possible for all I know if I have really no experience of greenness.

So we shouted at each other and shook the room because Metaphysics is the only thoroughly emotional thing. And the difference between us was very deep because it was a difference as to the object of the whole thing called broad-mindedness or the opening of the intellect.

For my friend said that he opened his intellect as the sun opens the fans of a palm tree, opening for opening's sake, opening infinitely for ever.

But I said that I opened my intellect as I opened my mouth in order to shut it again on something solid. I was doing it at the moment. And as I truly pointed out, it would look uncommonly silly if I went on opening my mouth infinitely, for ever and ever.

Now when this argument was over, or at least when it was cut short (for it will never be over), I went away with one of my companions who, in the confusion and comparative insanity of a General Election, had somehow become a Member of Parliament, and I drove with him in a cab from the corner of Leicester Square to the Members' entrance of the House of Commons, where the police received me with a quite unusual tolerance. Whether they thought that he was my keeper or that I was his keeper is a discussion between us which still continues.

It is necessary in this narrative to preserve the utmost exactitude of detail.

After leaving my friend at the House, I took the cab on a few hundred yards to an office in Victoria Street which I had to visit. I then got out and offered him more than his fare.

He looked at it, but not with the surly doubt and general disposition to try it on, which is not unknown among normal Cabmen. But this was no normal, perhaps, no human, Cabman. He looked at it with a dull and infantile astonishment, clearly quite genuine.

"Do you know, sir," he said, "you've only given me 1s. 8d?"

I remarked, with some surprise, that I did know it.

"Now you know, sir," said he in a kindly, appealing, reasonable way, "you know that ain't the fare from Euston."

"Euston," I repeated vaguely, for the phrase at that moment sounded to me like China or Arabia. "What on earth has Euston got to do with It?"

"You hailed me just outside Euston Station," began the man with astonishing precision, "and then you said...."

"What in the name of Tartarus are you talking about?" I said with Christian forbearance; "I took you at the southwest corner of Leicester Square."

"Leicester Square," he exclaimed, loosening a kind of cataract of scorn, "why we ain't been near Leicester Square today. You hailed me outside Euston Station, and you said...."

"Are you mad, or am I?" I asked with scientific calm.

I looked at the man.

No ordinary dishonest Cabman would think of creating so solid and colossal and creative a lie. And this man was not a dishonest Cabman. If ever a human face was heavy and simple and humble and, with great big blue eyes protruding like a frog's, if ever (in short) a human face was all that a human face should be, it was the face of that resentful and respectful Cabman.

I looked up and down the street; an unusually dark twilight seemed to be coming on. And for one second the old nightmare of the skeptic put its finger on my nerve. What was certainty? Was anybody certain of anything? Heavens! to think of the dull rut of the skeptics who go on asking whether we possess a future life. The exciting question for real skepticism is whether we possess past life. What is a minute ago, rationalistically considered, except a tradition and a picture?

The darkness grew deeper from the road. The Cabman calmly gave me the most elaborate details of the gesture, the words, the complex but consistent course of action which I had adopted since that remarkable occasion when I had hailed him outside Euston Station.

How did I know (my skeptical friends would say) that I had not hailed him outside Euston?

I was firm about my assertion; he was quite equally firm about his.

He was obviously quite as honest a man as I, and a member of a much more respectable profession.

In that moment the universe and the stars swung just a hair's breadth from their balance, and the foundations of the earth were moved.

But for the same reason that I believe in Democracy, for the same reason that I believe in Free Will, for the same reason that I believe in Fixed Character of Virtue, the reason that could only be expressed by saying that I do not choose to be a lunatic, I continued to believe that this honest Cabman was wrong, and I repeated to him that I had really taken him at the corner of Leicester Square.

He began with the same evident and ponderous sincerity, "You hailed me outside Euston Station, and you said...."

And at this moment there came over his features a kind of frightful transfiguration of living astonishment, as if he had been lit up like a lamp from the inside.

"Why, I beg your pardon, sir," he said. "I beg your pardon. I beg your pardon. You took me from Leicester Square. I remember now. I beg your pardon."

And with that, this astonishing man let out his whip with a sharp crack at his horse and went trundling away.

The whole of which interview, before the banner of St. George I swear, is strictly true.

I looked at the strange Cabman as he lessened in the distance and the mists.

I do not know whether I was right in fancying that although his face had seemed so honest, there was something unearthly and demoniac about him when seen from behind.

Perhaps he had been sent to tempt me from my adherence to those sanities and certainties which I had defended earlier in the day.

In any case it gave me pleasure to remember that my sense of reality, though it had rocked for an instant, had remained erect.

Soho: London district in which foreign restaurants were frequented by literary and artistic types, and businesses ranged from the more salubrious (street markets) to the less salubrious (street-walkers). *To my friend:* probably George Bernard Shaw. *My friend ... opened his intellect:* probably H. G. Wells. *Member of Parliament:* probably Hilaire Belloc, M.P. for Salford, 1906–10. *1s 8d:* 1 shilling 8 pence. *Euston:* one of London's many railway termini. *Tartarus:* Greek mythology for Hell. *Leicester Square:* ride to the Houses of Parliament was 1.16 miles. *Euston Station:* ride from Euston Station to the H of P was 2 miles. *Cabman was wrong:* Cabmen never believed they were wrong. *Source:* "The Extraordinary Cabman" first appeared in London's *Daily News.* It was later collected in the volume of essays *Tremendous Trifles,* 1909.

3

HABITS OF SOUL

THE VANITY OF VIRTUES AND VICES

Paradoxy: the impact of satiric cartoons from 1800 to 1900: bludgeon then, blush now. *Hilarity:* "Renaissance artists who mixed colors exquisitely mixed poisons equally exquisitely." *Humility:* one may be vain about virtues yet to be acquired; at the same time one may be humble about virtues already acquired. *Scripture:* "When you do do virtue, don't tell the world; God knows; that should be enough" (Matthew 6:34).

If a man must needs be conceited, it is certainly better that he should be conceited about some merits or talents that he does not really possess. For then his vanity remains more or less superficial; it remains a mere mistake of fact, like that of a man who thinks he inherits the royal blood or thinks he has an infallible system for Monte Carlo.

Because the merit is an unreal merit, it does not corrupt or sophisticate his real merits. He is vain about the virtue he has not got; but he may be humble about the virtues that he has got. His truly honorable qualities remain in their primordial innocence; he cannot see them, and he cannot spoil them. If a man's mind is erroneously possessed with the idea that he is a great violinist, that need not prevent his being a gentleman and an honest man.

But if once his mind is possessed in any strong degree with the knowledge that he is a gentleman, he will soon cease to be one.

But there is a third kind of satisfaction of which I have noticed one or two examples lately — another kind of satisfaction which is neither a pleasure in the virtues that we do possess nor a pleasure in the virtues we do not possess. It is the pleasure which a man takes in the presence or absence of certain things in himself without ever adequately asking himself whether in his case they constitute virtues at all.

A man will plume himself because he is not bad in some particular way when the truth is that he is not good enough to be bad in that particular way. Some priggish little clerk will say, "I have reason to congratulate myself that I am a civilized person, and not so bloodthirsty as the Mad Mullah." Somebody ought to say to him, "A really good man would be less bloodthirsty than the Mullah. But you are less bloodthirsty, not because you are more of a good man, but because you are a great deal less of a man. You are not bloodthirsty, not because you would spare your enemy, but because you would run away from him."

Or, again, some Puritan with a sullen type of piety would say, "I have reason to congratulate myself that I do not worship graven images like the old heathen Greeks." And again somebody ought to say to him, "The best religion may not worship graven images because it may see beyond them. But if you do not worship graven images, it is only because you are mentally and morally quite incapable of graving them. True religion, perhaps, is above idolatry. But you are below idolatry. You are not holy enough yet to worship a lump of stone."

In turning over a pile of newspapers, I noticed two cases of this confusion. In one case Mr. F. C. Gould, the brilliant and felicitous caricaturist, delivered a most interesting speech upon the nature and atmosphere of our modern English caricature.

I think there is really very little to congratulate oneself about in the condition of English caricature. There are few causes for pride. Probably the greatest cause for pride is Mr. F. C. Gould. But Mr. F. C. Gould, forbidden by modesty to adduce this excellent ground for optimism, fell back upon saying a thing which is said by numbers of other people, but has not perhaps been said lately with the full authority of an eminent cartoonist.

He said that he thought "that they might congratulate themselves that the style of caricature which found acceptation nowadays was very different from the lampoon of the old days."

Continuing, he said, according to the newspaper report, "On looking back to the political lampoons of Rowlandson's and Gillray's time, they would find them coarse and brutal. In some countries abroad still, 'even in America,' the method of political caricature was of the bludgeon kind. The fact was we had passed the bludgeon stage. If they were brutal in attacking a man, even for political reasons, they roused sympathy for the man who was attacked. What they had to do was to rub in the point they wanted to emphasize as gently as they could." (*Laughter and applause.*)

Anybody reading these words, and anybody who heard them, will certainly feel that there is in them a great deal of truth, as well as a great deal of geniality. But along with that truth and with that geniality there is a streak of that erroneous type of optimism which is founded on the fallacy of which I have spoken above. Before we congratulate ourselves upon the absence of certain faults from our nation or society, we ought to ask ourselves why it is that these faults are absent.

Are we without the fault because we have the opposite virtue?

Or are we without the fault because we have the opposite fault?

It is a good thing assuredly, to be innocent of any excess; but let us be sure that we are not innocent of excess merely by being guilty of defect.

Is it really true that our English political satire is so moderate because it is so magnanimous, so forgiving, so saintly?

Is it penetrated through and through with a mystical charity, with a psychological tenderness?

Do we spare the feelings of the Cabinet Minister because we pierce through all his apparent crimes and follies down to the dark virtues of which his own soul is unaware?

Do we temper the wind to the Leader of the Opposition because in our all-embracing heart we pity and cherish the struggling spirit of the Leader of the Opposition?

Briefly, have we left off being brutal because we are too grand and generous to be brutal?

Is it really true that we are *better* than brutality?

Is it really true that we have *passed* the bludgeon stage?

I fear that there is, to say the least of it, another side to the matter. Is it not only too probable that the mildness of our political satire, when compared with the political satire of our fathers, arises simply from the profound unreality of our current politics? Rowlandson and Gillray did not fight merely because they were naturally pothouse pugilists; they fought because they had something to fight about. It is easy enough to be refined about things that do not matter; but men kicked and plunged a little in that portentous wrestle in which swung to and fro, alike dizzy with danger, the independence of England, the independence of Ireland, the independence of France.

If we wish for a proof of this fact that the lack of refinement did not come from mere brutality, the proof is easy. The proof is that in that struggle no personalities were more brutal than the really refined personalities. None were more violent and intolerant than those who were by nature polished and sensitive. Nelson, for instance, had the nerves and good manners of a woman; nobody in his sense, I suppose, would call Nelson "brutal." But when he was touched upon the national matter, there sprang out of him a spout of oaths, and he could only tell men to "Kill! kill! kill the d — d Frenchmen."

It would be as easy to take examples on the other side. Camille Desmoulins was a man of much the same type, not only elegant and sweet in temper, but almost tremulously tender and humanitarian. But he was ready, he said, "to embrace Liberty upon a pile of corpses." In Ireland there were even more instances. Robert Emmet was only one famous example of a whole family of men at once sensitive and savage.

I think that Mr. F. C. Gould is altogether wrong in talking of this political ferocity as if it were some sort of survival from ruder conditions, like a flint axe or a hairy man. Cruelty is, perhaps, the worst kind of sin. Intellectual cruelty is certainly the worst kind of cruelty. But there is nothing in the least barbaric or ignorant about intellectual cruelty. The great Renaissance artists who mixed colors exquisitely mixed poisons equally exquisitely. The great Renaissance princes who designed instruments of music also designed instruments of torture. Barbarity, malignity, the desire to hurt men, are the evil things generated in atmospheres of intense reality when great nations or great causes are at war. We may, perhaps, be glad that we have not got them, but it is somewhat dangerous to be proud that we have not got them. Perhaps we are hardly great enough to have them.

Perhaps some great virtues have to be generated, as in men like Nelson or Emmet before we can have these vices at all, even as temptations. I, for one, believe that if our caricaturists do not hate their enemies, it is not because they are too big to hate them, but because their enemies are not big enough to hate. I do not think we have passed the bludgeon stage. I believe we have not come to the bludgeon stage. We must be better, braver, and purer men than we are before we come to the bludgeon stage.

Let us then, by all means, be proud of the virtues that we have not got; but let us not be too arrogant about the virtues that we cannot help having. It may be that a man living on a desert island has a right to congratulate himself upon the fact that he can meditate at his ease. But he must not congratulate himself on the fact that he is on a desert island, and at the same time congratulate himself on the self-restraint he shows in not going to a ball every night.

Similarly our England may have a right to congratulate itself upon the fact that her politics are very quiet, amicable, and humdrum. But she must not congratulate herself upon that fact and also congratulate herself upon the self-restraint she shows in not tearing herself and her citizens into rags.

Between two English Privy Councillors polite language is a mark of civilization, but really not a mark of magnanimity.

Allied to this question is the kindred question on which we so often hear an innocent British boast the fact that our statesmen are privately on very friendly relations, although in Parliament they sit on opposite sides of the House. Here, again, it is as well to have no illusions. Our statesmen are not monsters of mystical generosity or insane logic who are really able to hate a man from three to twelve and to love him from twelve to three.

If our social relations are more peaceful than those of France or America or the England of a hundred years ago, it is simply because our politics are more peaceful, not improbably because our politics are more fictitious. If our statesmen agree more in private, it is for the very simple reason that they agree more in public. And the reason that they agree so much in both cases is really that they belong to one social class and, therefore, the dining life is the real life. Tory and Liberal statesmen like each other, but it is not because they are both expansive; it is because they are both exclusive.

Monte Carlo: resort-cum-gambling casino in Monaco. *Francis Carruthers Gould* (1844–1925): first staff cartoonist in English journalism. *Brilliant and felicitous caricaturist:* Chesterton could have been one himself if he hadn't dropped out of the Slade. *Thomas Rowlandson* (1756–1827): English painter and rowdy caricaturist whose hallmark seemed to be enormous bosoms and bottoms. *James Gillray* (1756–1815): English caricaturist chiefly remembered for lively political cartoons directed against George III and Napoleon I. *Horatio Lord Nelson* (1758–1805): fabled admiral during the French wars; favored lover of Emma, Lady Hamilton during a touching love affair; he was killed by enemy fire on HMS *Victory*. *Pothouse:* small tavern or public house. *Camille Desmoulins* (1760–94): careless French revolutionist and journalist who himself fell to the guillotine. *Robert Emmet* (1764–1827): Irish patriot who led a short-lived outbreak in Dublin in 1803, for which he was later executed. *Source:* Originally published under the title "Real Virtues or Opposite Faults?" *The Illustrated London News,* December 30, 1905; as it appears in CW27, 87–91.

THE PARADOX OF VIRTUES AND VICES

Paradoxy, Hilarity, Humility: "The secret of life lies in Laughter and Humility." *Scripture:* "In spring time the green grasses come" (VUL Zecharias 10:1; NRSV Zechariah 10:1). *Scripture:* "At harvest time the green grasses go" (VUL Isaias 40:6–9; NRSV Isaiah 40:6–9).

The tradition of Christianity (which is still the only coherent ethic of Europe) rests on two or three paradoxes or mysteries which can easily be impugned in argument and as easily justified in life.

One of them, for instance, is the Paradox of Hope or Faith, that the more hopeless is the situation, the more hopeful must be the man....

Another is the Paradox of Charity or Chivalry, that the weaker a thing is, the more it should be respected; that the more indefensible a thing is, the more it should appeal to us for a certain kind of defense....

Now, one of these very practical and working mysteries in the Christian tradition, and one which the Roman Catholic Church, as I say, has done her best work in singling out, is the conception of the sinfulness of Pride. Pride is a weakness in the character; it dries up laughter, it dries up wonder, it dries up chivalry and energy....

For the Truth is much stranger even than it appears in the formal doctrine of the sin of Pride. It is not only true that Humility is a much wiser and more vigorous thing than Pride. It is also true that Vanity is a much wiser and more vigorous thing than Pride. Vanity is social; it is almost a kind of comradeship — Pride is solitary and uncivilized. Vanity is active; it desires the applause of infinite multitudes — Pride is passive, desiring only the applause of one person, which it already has. Vanity is humorous, and can enjoy the joke even of itself — Pride is dull, and cannot even smile....

The secret of life lies in Laughter and Humility. Self is the gorgon. Vanity sees it in the mirror of other men and lives — Pride studies it for itself and is turned to stone....

One of the thousand objections to the sin of Pride lies precisely in this, that self-consciousness of necessity destroys self-revelation. A man who thinks a great deal about himself will try to be many-sided, attempt a theatrical excellence at all points, will try to be an encyclopedia of culture, and his own real personality will be lost in that false universalism. Thinking about himself will lead to trying to be the universe; trying to be the universe will lead to ceasing to be anything. If, on the other hand, a man is sensible enough to think only about the universe; he will think about it in his own individual way. He will keep virgin the secret of God; he will see the grass as no other man can see it, and look at a sun that no man has ever known.

Paradoxes: the New Testament abounds in paradoxes of all kinds. The yoke is sweet. The first shall be last. The seed has to die if it's to live again. Lose your life if ever you expect to find it again. *Source:* Excerpt from "The Moods of Mr. George Moore," chapter 9 of *Heretics,* 1905; as it appears in cw1, 106–9.

THE NIGHTMARE

Paradoxy: Idols are false, dolls are true. *Hilarity:* There's nothing so delightful as a nightmare, especially when you know it's a nightmare. *Humility:* Certain sanctities, true possessions, should be "Christian and simple." *Scripture:* " 'Where did all these funny little gods come from anyway?' asked Jacob of his household. 'Sweep them up and toss them out! Then a nice bath, a change of clothes, and we're off. Up to Bethel. That's where we'll make an altar to God. The One who came to me when I had my troubles. He's been with me ever since' " (Genesis 35:2–3).

A sunset of copper and gold had just broken down and gone to pieces in the west, and gray colors were crawling over everything in earth and heaven. Also a wind was growing, a wind that laid a cold finger upon flesh and spirit. The bushes at the back of my garden began to whisper like conspirators, and then to wave like wild hands in signal.

I was trying to read by the last light that died on the lawn a long poem of the decadent period, a poem about the old gods of Babylon and Egypt, about their blazing and obscene temples, their cruel and colossal faces.

> Or didst thou love the God of Flies
> who plagued the Hebrews and was splashed
> With wine unto the waist, or Pasht
> who had green beryls for her eyes?

I read this poem because I had to review it for the *Daily News;* still it was genuine poetry of its kind. It really gave out an atmosphere, a fragrant and suffocating smoke that seemed really to come from the Bondage of Egypt or the Burden of Tyre.

There is not much in common (thank God) between my garden with the gray-green English skyline beyond it, and these mad visions of painted palaces, huge headless idols, and monstrous solitudes of red or golden sand. Nevertheless, as I confessed to myself, I can fancy in such a stormy twilight some such smell of death and fear.

The ruined sunset really looks like one of their ruined temples, a shattered heap of gold and green marble. A black flapping thing detaches itself from one of the somber trees and flutters to another. I know not if it is owl or flittermouse; I could fancy it was a black cherub, an infernal cherub of darkness, not with the wings of a bird and the head of a baby, but with the head of a goblin and the wings of a bat.

I think, if there were light enough, I could sit here and write some very creditable creepy tale about how I went up the crooked road beyond the church and met Something — say a dog, a dog with one eye.

Then I should meet a horse, perhaps, a horse without a rider; the horse also would have one eye.

Then the inhuman silence would be broken; I should meet a man — need I say, a one-eyed man? — who would ask me the way to my own house.

Or perhaps tell me that it was burned to the ground.

I think I could tell a very cozy little tale along some such lines.

Or I might dream of climbing for ever the tall dark trees above me. They are so tall that I feel as if I should find at their tops the nests of the angels; but in this mood they would be dark and dreadful angels; angels of death.

Only, you see, this mood is all bosh. I do not believe it in the least. That one-eyed universe, with its one-eyed men and beasts, was only created with one universal wink. At the top of the tragic trees I should not find the Angel's Nest. I should only find the Mare's Nest; the dreamy and divine nest is not there. In the Mare's Nest I shall discover that dim, enormous opalescent egg from which is hatched the Nightmare. For there is nothing so delightful as a nightmare — when you know it is a nightmare.

That is the essential. That is the stern condition laid upon all artists touching this luxury of fear. The terror must be fundamentally frivolous. Sanity may play with insanity — but insanity must not be allowed to play with sanity. Let such poets as the one I was reading in the garden, by all means, be free to imagine what outrageous deities and violent landscapes they like. By all means let them wander freely amid their opium pinnacles and perspectives.

But these huge gods, these high cities, are toys; they must never for an instant be allowed to be anything else. Man, a gigantic child, must play with Babylon and Nineveh, with Isis and with Ashtaroth. By all means let him dream of the Bondage of Egypt so long as he is free from it. By all means let him take up the Burden of Tyre so long as he can take it lightly. But the old gods must be his dolls, not his idols.

His central sanctities, his true possessions, should be Christian and simple. And just as a child would cherish most a wooden horse or a sword that is a mere cross of wood, so man, the great child, must cherish most the old plain things of poetry and piety; that horse of wood that was the epic end of Ilium, or that cross of wood that redeemed and conquered the world.

In one of Stevenson's letters there is a characteristically humorous remark about the appalling impression produced on him in childhood by the beasts with many eyes in the Book of Revelations. "If that was Heaven, what in the name of Davy Jones was Hell like?"

Now in sober truth there is a magnificent idea in these monsters of the Apocalypse. It is, I suppose, the idea that beings really more beautiful or more universal than we are might appear to us frightful and even confused. Especially they might seem to have senses at once more multiplex and more staring; an idea very imaginatively seized in the multitude of eyes.

I like those monsters beneath the throne very much. It is when one of them goes wandering in deserts and finds a throne for himself that evil faiths begin, and there is, literally, the Devil to pay — to pay in dancing girls or human sacrifice. As long as those misshapen elemental powers are around the throne, remember that the thing that they worship is the likeness of the appearance of a man.

That is, I fancy, the true doctrine on the subject of *Tales of Terror* and such things, which unless a man of letters do well and truly believe, without doubt he will end by blowing his brains out or by writing badly. Man, the central pillar of the world, must be upright and straight; around him all the trees and beasts and elements and devils may crook and curl like smoke if they choose.

All really imaginative literature is only the contrast between the weird curves of Nature and the straightness of the Soul. Man may behold what ugliness he likes if he is sure that he will not worship it; but there are some so weak that they will worship a thing only because it is ugly. These must be chained to the beautiful. It is not always wrong even to go, like Dante, to the brink of the lowest promontory and look down at Hell. It is when you look up at Hell that a serious miscalculation has probably been made.

Therefore, I see no wrong in riding with the Nightmare tonight.

She whinnies to me from the rocking treetops and the roaring wind.

I will catch her and ride her through the awful air.

Woods and weeds are alike tugging at the roots in the rising tempest, as if all wished to fly with us over the moon, like that wild, amorous cow whose child was the Moon-Calf.

We will rise to that mad infinite where there is neither up nor down, the high topsy-turvydom of the heavens.

I will ride on the Nightmare — but she shall not ride on me.

Flittermouse: bat. *Mare's Nest:* discovery that proves to be illusory. *Source:* Chapter in GKC's *Alarms and Discursions* (New York: Dodd, Mead, 1911 [1910]) as it appears in e-text.

A PIECE OF CHALK

Paradoxy: White isn't the absence of color; it's a full-blown color itself. Nor is virtue the absence of vice; virtue is a vivid and separate thing, like a particular pain, smell, color. *Hilarity:* "When a cow came slouching by in a field next to me, a mere artist might have drawn it; but I always get wrong in the hind legs of quadrupeds."

Humility: virtue is alive and well and on the hoof. *Scripture:* "Congratulate me! I've found the white chalk I was looking for!" (Luke 15:9).

I remember one splendid morning, all blue and silver, in the summer holidays when I reluctantly tore myself away from the task of doing nothing in particular, and put on a hat of some sort and picked up a walking stick, and put six very bright-colored chalks in my pocket.

I then went into the kitchen (which along with the rest of the house, belonged to a very square and sensible woman in a Sussex village), and asked the owner and occupant of the kitchen if she had any brown paper. She had a great deal; in fact she had too much; and she mistook the purpose and the rationale of the existence of brown paper.

She seemed to have an idea that if a person wanted brown paper, he must be wanting to tie up parcels, which was the last thing I wanted to do; indeed it is a thing which I have found to be beyond my mental capacity. Hence, she dwelled very much on the varying qualities of toughness and endurance in the material.

I explained to her that I only wanted to draw pictures on it, and that I did not want them to endure in the least; and that from my point of view, therefore, it was a question, not of tough consistency, but of responsive surface, a thing comparatively irrelevant in a parcel.

When she understood that I wanted to draw, she offered to overwhelm me with notepaper, apparently supposing that I did my notes and correspondence on old brown paper wrappers from motives of economy.

I then tried to explain the rather delicate logical shade that I not only like brown paper, but I liked the quality of brownness in paper, just as I liked the quality of brownness in October woods, or in beer, or in the peat streams of the North.

Brown paper represents the primal twilight of the first toil of creation and, with a bright-colored chalk or two, you can pick out points of fire in it, sparks of gold, and blood-red, and sea-green, like the first fierce stars that sprang out of divine darkness.

All this I said, in an off-hand way, to the old woman; and I put the brown paper in my pocket along with the chalks, and possibly other things. I suppose everyone must have reflected how primeval and how poetical are the things that one carries in one's pocket; the pocketknife, for instance, the type of all human tools, the infant of the sword. Once I planned to write a book of poems entirely about the things in my pockets. But I found it was too long, and the age of great epics is past.

With my stick, my knife, my chalks, and my brown paper, I went out on to the great downs. I crawled across those colossal contours that express the best quality of England because they are at the same time soft and strong. The smoothness of them has the same meaning as the smoothness of great cart horses, or the smoothness of the beech tree; it declares in the teeth of our timid and cruel theories that the mighty are merciful.

As my eye swept the landscape, the landscape was as kindly as any of its cottages, but for power it was like an earthquake. The villages in the immense valley were safe, one could see, for centuries; yet the lifting of the whole land was like the lifting of one enormous wave to wash them all away.

I crossed one swell of living turf after another, looking for a place to sit down and draw. Do not, for Heaven's sake, imagine I was going to sketch from Nature. I was going to draw Devils and Seraphim, and Blind Old Gods that men worshiped before the dawn of right, and Saints in robes of angry crimson, and seas of strange green, and all the Sacred or Monstrous Symbols that look so well in bright colors on brown drawing paper. They are much better worth drawing than Nature; also they are much easier to draw.

When a cow came slouching by in a field next to me, a mere artist might have drawn it; but I always get wrong in the hind legs of quadrupeds. So I drew the soul of the cow, which I saw there plainly walking before me in the sunlight; and the soul was all purple and silver, and had seven horns and the mystery that belongs to all beasts.

But though I could not with a crayon get the best out of the landscape, it does not follow that the landscape was not getting the best out of me. And this, I think, is the mistake that people make about the old poets who lived before Wordsworth and were supposed not to care very much about Nature because they did not describe it much.

They preferred writing about great men to writing about great hills; but they sat on the great hills to write about it. They gave out much less about Nature, but they drank it in, perhaps, much more. They painted the white robes of their Holy Virgins with the blinding snow at which they had stared all day. They blazoned the shields of their paladins with the purple and gold of many heraldic sunsets. The greenness of a thousand green leaves clustered into the live green figure of Robin Hood. The blueness of a score of forgotten skies became the blue robes of the Virgin. The inspiration went in like sunbeams and came out like Apollo.

But as I sat scrawling these silly figures on the brown paper, it began to dawn on me, to my great disgust, that I had left one chalk, and that a most exquisite and essential chalk, behind. I searched all of my pockets, but I could not find any white chalk.

Now, those who are acquainted with Philosophy (nay, Religion) which is typified in the art of drawing on brown paper, know that white is positive and essential. I cannot avoid remarking here on a moral significance.

One of the wise and awful truths which this brown-paper art reveals is this, that white is a color. It is not a mere absence of color; it is a shining and affirmative thing, as fierce as red, as definite as black. When, so to speak, your pencil grows red-hot, it draws roses; when it grows white-hot, it draws stars.

And one of the two or three defiant verities of the best religious morality, of real Christianity, for example, is exactly this same thing. The chief assertion of religious morality is that white is a color. Virtue is not the absence of vices or the avoidance of moral dangers. Virtue is a vivid and separate thing, like pain or a particular smell.

Mercy does not mean not being cruel or sparing people revenge or punishment; it means a plain and positive thing like the sun, which one has either seen or not seen.

Chastity does not mean abstention from sexual wrong; it means something flaming, like Joan of Arc.

In a word, God paints in many colors; but He never paints so gorgeously, I had almost said so gaudily, as when He paints in white.

In a sense our age has realized this fact and expressed it in our sullen costume. For if it were really true that white was a blank and colorless thing, negative and noncommittal, then white would be used instead of black and gray for the funeral of this pessimistic period. We should see city gentlemen in frock coats of spotless silver linen, with top hats as white as wonderful arum lilies. Which is not the case.

Meanwhile, I could not find my chalk.

I sat on the hill in a sort of despair. There was no town nearer than Chichester at which it was even remotely probable that there would be such a thing as an artist's colorman. And yet, without white, my absurd little pictures would have been as pointless as the world would be if there were no good people in it. I stared stupidly round, racking my brain for expedients.

Then I suddenly stood and roared with laughter, again and again, so that the cows stared at me and called a committee. Imagine a man in the Sahara regretting that he had no sand for his hourglass. Imagine a gentleman in mid-ocean wishing that he had brought some salt water with him for some chemical experiment.

I was sitting in an immense warehouse of white chalk. The landscape was made entirely out of white chalk. White chalk was piled more miles until it met the sky.

I stooped and broke a piece off the rock I sat on. It did not mark so well as the shop chalks do, but it gave the effect.

And I stood there in a trance of pleasure, realizing that this Southern England is not only a grand peninsula and a tradition and a civilization.

It is something even more admirable.

It is a piece of chalk.

Sussex: southeastern England, a sandstone area of hilly grasslands and woodlands in the north, across undulating grasslands of the river valleys in the center, to the steep chalk scarps of the north-facing South Downs in the extreme south, inland from the English Channel. *Brown paper:* Chesterton often lined a wall of his residence with brown paper, in anticipation of sudden inspiration, to draw on in chalk or crayon. *Great Downs:* open tracts of high ground; treeless undulating chalk uplands of south and southeast England and elsewhere, traditionally a major source of pasturage. *Paladins:* the twelve bravest and most famous warriors of Charlemagne's court; knights errant; champions. *Robin Hood:* legendary outlaw hero of a series of English ballads, some of which date from the fourteenth century; the hangout for him and his furtive men was a forest, Sherwood Forest. *Apollo:* sun god of the ancient Greeks and Romans. *White ... instead of black and gray:* and so it has come to pass at the end of the twentieth century, white as the funereal color, symbolic of the Resurrection and the Life. *Chichester:* city lying on the coastal plain of the English Channel at the foot of the chalk South Downs a mile from the head of Chichester Harbour, with which it is connected by canal. *Colorman:* purveyor of artist's supplies. *Source:* A chapter in *Tremendous Trifles,* 1909.

4

HABITS OF OBSERVANCE

LOVE THY GOD

Paradoxy: The Christian Church is to the State what Sherlock Holmes was to Scotland Yard, a private consulting detective who will set the record straight. *Hilarity:* The Church pursues miscreants, not to punish, but to pardon, them. *Humility:* Truth can be found merely by referring to vulgar literature — its unfailing fountain. *Scripture:* "Take me by the hand, O Lord, and lead me down the path of truth" (Psalm 85:11 VUL; 86:11 NRSV).

Every person of sound education enjoys detective stories, and there are even several points on which they have a hearty superiority to most modern books. A detective story generally describes six living men discussing how it is that a man is dead. A modern philosophic story generally describes six dead men discussing how any man can possibly be alive.

But those who have enjoyed the *roman policier* must have noted one thing, that when the murderer is caught he is hardly ever hanged. "That," says Sherlock Holmes, "is the advantage of being a private detective"; after he has caught, he can set free.

The Christian Church can best be defined as an enormous private detective, correcting that official detective — the State.

This, indeed, is one of the injustices done to historic Christianity; injustices which arise from looking at complex exceptions and not at the large and simple fact. We are constantly being told that Theologians used racks and thumbscrews, and so they did. Theologians used racks and thumbscrews just as they used thimbles and three-legged stools because everybody else used them. Christianity no more created the medieval tortures than it did the Chinese tortures; it inherited them from any empire as heathen as the Chinese. The Church did, in an evil hour, consent to imitate the commonwealth and employ cruelty.

But if we open our eyes and take in the whole picture, if we look at the general shape and color of the thing, the real difference between the Church and the State is huge and plain. The State, in all lands and ages, has created a machinery of punishment, more bloody and brutal in some places than others, but bloody and brutal everywhere. The Church is the only institution that ever attempted to create a machinery of pardon.

The Church is the only thing that ever attempted by system to pursue and discover crimes, not in order to avenge, but in order to forgive them. The stake and rack were merely the weaknesses of the religion; its snobberies, its surrenders to the world. Its speciality — or, if you like, its oddity — was this merciless mercy; the unrelenting sleuthhound who seeks to save and not slay....

Roman policier: French for "detective novel," a literary genre fathered in France by Émile Gaboriau (c. 1835–1873); he has been described as the Edgar Allen Poe of France; his detective Monsieur Lecoq was a fictional precursor of Sherlock Holmes. *Source:* "The Divine Detective," a chapter in *A Miscellany of Men,* 1912.

LOVE THY NEIGHBOR

Paradoxy: Because our neighbor "may be anybody, he is everybody." *Hilarity:* Friends and enemies are our own doing, but God has to take credit for our neighbors. *Humility:* "We have to love our neighbor because he is there." *Scripture:* "Love thy neighbor"

(Matthew 5:43, 19:19, 22:39; Mark 12:31; Luke 10:27; Romans 13:9; Galatians 5:14; James 2:8).

We make our friends; we make our enemies; but God makes our next-door neighbor. Hence he comes to us clad in all the careless terrors of nature. He is as strange as the stars, as reckless and indifferent as the rain. He is Man, the most terrible of the beasts. That is why the old religions and the old scriptural language showed so sharp a wisdom when they spoke, not of one's duty toward humanity, but one's duty toward one's neighbor.

The duty toward humanity may often take the form of some choice which is personal or even pleasurable. That duty may be a hobby; it may even be a dissipation. We may work in the East End because we are peculiarly fitted to work in the East End, or because we think we are; we may fight for the cause of international peace because we are very fond of fighting.

The most monstrous martyrdom, the most repulsive experience, may be the result of choice or a kind of taste. We may be so made as to be particularly fond of lunatics or specially interested in leprosy. We may love Negroes because they are black or German Socialists because they are pedantic.

But we have to love our neighbor because he is there — a much more alarming reason for a much more serious operation. He is the sample of humanity which is actually given us. Precisely because he may be anybody, he is everybody. He is a symbol because he is an accident.

East End: area of London perennially crowded with immigrants. *Source:* Excerpt from "On Certain Modern Writers and the Institution of the Family," chapter 14 of *Heretics,* CW1, 139–40.

LOVE THY FAMILY

Paradoxy: "It is a good thing for a man to live in a family for the same reason that it is a good thing for a man to be besieged in a city." *Hilarity:* "It is a good thing for a man to live in a family in the same sense that it is a beautiful and delightful thing for a man to be snowed up in a street." *Humility:* "Life, if it be a truly stimulating and fascinating life, is a thing which, of its nature, exists in spite of ourselves." *Scripture:* "You're no longer permanent guests or new arrivals in our family on earth. Along with the saints you're now members of the family of God" (Ephesians 2:19).

Doubtless men flee from small environments into lands that are very deadly. But this is natural enough, for they are not fleeing from death. They are fleeing from life. And this principle applies to ring within ring of the social system of humanity. It is perfectly reasonable that men should seek for some particular variety of the human type, so long as they are seeking for that variety of the human type and not for mere human variety.

It is quite proper that a British diplomatist should seek the society of Japanese generals if what he wants is Japanese generals. But if what he wants is people different from himself, he had much better stop at home and discuss religion with the housemaid.

It is quite reasonable that the village genius should come up to conquer London if what he wants is to conquer London. But if he wants to conquer something fundamentally and symbolically hostile and also very strong, he had much better remain where he is and have a row with the rector.

The man in the suburban street is quite right if he goes to Ramsgate for the sake of Ramsgate — a difficult thing to imagine. But if, as he expresses it, he goes to Ramsgate "for a change," then he would have a much more romantic and even melodramatic change if he jumped over the wall into his neighbor's garden. The consequences would be bracing in a sense far beyond the possibilities of Ramsgate hygiene.

Now, exactly as this principle applies to the empire, to the nation within the empire, to the city within the nation, to the street within the city, so it applies to the home within the street. The institution of the family is to be commended for precisely the same reasons that the institution of the nation, or the institution of the city, are in this matter to be commended.

It is a good thing for a man to live in a family for the same reason that it is a good thing for a man to be besieged in a city. It is a good thing for a man to live in a family in the same sense that it is a beautiful and delightful thing for a man to be snowed up in a street. They all force him to realize that life is not a thing from outside, but a thing from inside. Above all, they all insist upon the fact that life, if it be a truly stimulating and fascinating life, is a thing which, of its nature, exists in spite of ourselves.

The modern writers who have suggested, in a more or less open manner, that the family is a bad institution, have generally confined themselves to suggesting, with much sharpness, bitterness, or pathos, that perhaps the family is not always very congenial. Of course the family is a good institution because it is uncongenial. It is wholesome precisely because it contains so many divergencies and varieties. It is, as the sentimentalists say, like a little kingdom and, like most other little kingdoms, is generally in a state of something resembling anarchy.

It is exactly because our brother George is not interested in our religious difficulties, but is interested in the Trocadero Restaurant, that the family has some of the bracing qualities of the commonwealth. It is precisely because our uncle Henry does not approve of the theatrical ambitions of our sister Sarah that the family is like humanity.

The men and women who, for good reasons and bad, revolt against the family are, for good reasons and bad, simply revolting against mankind. Aunt Elizabeth is unreasonable, like mankind. Papa is excitable, like mankind. Our youngest brother is mischievous, like mankind. Grandpapa is stupid, like the world; he is old, like the world.

Those who wish, rightly or wrongly, to step out of all this, do definitely wish to step into a narrower world. They are dismayed and terrified by the largeness and variety of the family. Sarah wishes to find a world wholly consisting of private theatricals; George wishes to think the Trocadero a cosmos.

I do not say, for a moment, that the flight to this narrower life may not be the right thing for the individual any more than I say the same thing about flight into a monastery. But I do say that anything is bad and artificial which tends to make these people succumb to the strange delusion that they are stepping into a world which is actually larger and more varied than their own.

The best way that a man could test his readiness to encounter the common variety of mankind would be to climb down a chimney into any house at random and get on as well as possible with the people inside. And that is essentially what each one of us did on the day that he was born.

This is, indeed, the sublime and special romance of the family. It is romantic because it is a toss-up. It is romantic because it is everything that its enemies call it. It is romantic because it is arbitrary. It is romantic because it is there.

So long as you have groups of men chosen rationally, you have some special or sectarian atmosphere. It is when you have groups of men chosen irrationally that you have men. The element of adventure begins to exist; for an adventure is, by its nature, a thing that comes to us. It is a thing that chooses us, not a thing that we choose.

Falling in love has been often regarded as the supreme adventure, the supreme romantic accident. In so much as there is in it something outside ourselves, something of a sort of merry fatalism, this is very true. Love does take us and transfigure and torture us. It does break our hearts with an unbearable beauty, like the unbearable beauty of music.

But in so far as we have certainly something to do with the matter; in so far as we are in some sense prepared to fall in love and in some sense jump into it; in so far as we do to some extent choose and to some extent even judge — in all this falling in love is not truly romantic, is not truly adventurous at all. In this degree the supreme adventure is not falling in love.

The supreme adventure is being born. There we do walk suddenly into a splendid and startling trap. There we do see something of which we have not dreamed before. Our father and mother do lie in wait for us and leap out on us, like brigands from a bush. Our uncle is a surprise. Our aunt is, in the beautiful common expression, a bolt from the blue.

When we step into the family, by the act of being born, we do step into a world which is incalculable, into a world which has its own strange laws, into a world which could do without us, into a world that we have not made. In other words, when we step into the family, we step into a Fairy Tale.

> *Ramsgate:* resort on the Strait of Dover four miles south of Margate; both popular resorts where saltwater swimming was touted for its hygienic effects. *Source:* Excerpt from "On Certain Modern Writers and the Institution of the Family," chapter 14 of *Heretics,* CW1, 140–43.

THE NEGATIVE SPIRIT

> *Paradoxy:* "This advantage the mystic morality must always have — it is always jollier." *Hilarity:* "A picture of a drunkard's liver would be more efficacious in the matter of temperance than any prayer or praise." *Humility:* "Visionary religion is, in one sense, necessarily more wholesome than our modern and reasonable morality." *Scripture:* "Dearly Beloved, I pray that all of you may thrive it happily and healthily in body and soul" (3 John 2).

Much has been said, and said truly, of the monkish morbidity, of the hysteria which has often gone with the visions of hermits or nuns. But let us never forget that this visionary religion is, in one sense, necessarily more wholesome than our modern and reasonable morality. It is more wholesome for this reason, that it can contemplate the idea of success or triumph in the hopeless fight toward the ethical ideal....

A modern morality, on the other hand, can only point with absolute conviction to the horrors that follow breaches of law; its only certainty is a certainty of ill. It can only point to imperfection. It has no perfection to point to. But the monk meditating upon Christ or Buddha has in his mind an image of perfect health, a thing of clear colors and clean air. He may contemplate this ideal wholeness and happiness far more than he ought; he may contemplate it to the neglect or exclusion of essential things; he may contemplate it until he has become a dreamer or a driveler; but still it is wholeness and happiness that he is contemplating. He may even go mad; but he is going mad for the love of sanity. But the modern student of ethics, even if he remains sane, remains sane from an insane dread of insanity.

The anchorite rolling on the stones in a frenzy of submission is a healthier person fundamentally than many a sober man in a silk hat who is walking down Cheapside. For many such are good only through a withering knowledge of evil. I am not at this moment claiming for the devotee anything more than this primary advantage, that though he may be making himself personally weak and miserable, he is still fixing his thoughts largely on gigantic strength and happiness, on a strength that has no limits, and a happiness that has no end. Doubtless there are other objections which can be urged without unreason against the influence of gods and visions in morality, whether in the cell or street. But this advantage the mystic morality must always have — it is always jollier. A young man may keep himself from vice by continually thinking of disease. He may keep himself from it also by continually thinking of the Virgin Mary. There may be question about which method is the more reasonable, or even about which is the more efficient. But surely there can be no question about which is the more wholesome.

I remember a pamphlet by that able and sincere secularist, Mr. G. W. Foote, which contained a phrase sharply symbolizing and dividing these two methods. The pamphlet was called "Beer and Bible," those two very noble things, all the nobler for a conjunction which Mr. Foote, in his stern old Puritan way, seemed to think sardonic, but which I confess to thinking appropriate and charming. I have not the work by me, but I remember that

Mr. Foote dismissed very contemptuously any attempts to deal with the problem of strong drink by religious offices or intercessions, and said that a picture of a drunkard's liver would be more efficacious in the matter of temperance than any prayer or praise. In that picturesque expression, it seems to me, is perfectly embodied the incurable morbidity of modern ethics. In that temple the lights are low, the crowds kneel, the solemn anthems are uplifted. But that upon the altar to which all men kneel is no longer the perfect flesh, the body and substance of the perfect man; it is still flesh, but it is diseased. It is the Drunkard's Liver of the New Testament that is marred for us, which we take in remembrance of Him.

Cheapside: A street in the City (the financial district) of London.
Source: Excerpt from chapter 2, "On the Negative Spirit," *Heretics;* as it appears in CW1, 47–49.

THOUGHTFUL JOKES

Paradoxy: "To take a thing and make a joke out of it is not to take it in vain." *Hilarity:* "The same book which says that God's name must not be taken vainly, talks easily and carelessly about God laughing and God winking." *Humility:* "The thing which is fundamentally and really frivolous is not a careless joke." *Scripture:* "God may have winked at ignorance in the past, but now He urges penance" (Acts 17:30).

Numbers of clergymen have from time to time reproached me for making jokes about religion; and they have almost always invoked the authority of that very sensible commandment which says, "Thou shalt not take the name of the Lord thy God in vain."

Of course, I pointed out that I was not in any conceivable sense taking the name in vain. To take a thing and make a joke out of it is not to take it in vain. It is, on the contrary, to take it and use it for an uncommonly good object. To use a thing in vain means to use it without use. But a joke may be exceedingly useful; it may contain the whole earthly sense, not to mention the whole heavenly sense, of a situation.

And those who find in the Bible the commandment can find in the Bible any number of the jokes. In the same book in which God's name is fenced from being taken in vain, God himself overwhelms Job with a torrent of terrible levities. The same book which says that God's name must not be taken vainly, talks easily and carelessly about God laughing and God winking. Evidently, it is not here that we have to look for genuine examples of what is meant by a vain use of the name.

And it is not very difficult to see where we have really to look for it. The people (as I tactfully pointed out to them) who really take the name of the Lord in vain are the clergymen themselves. The thing which is fundamentally and really frivolous is not a careless joke. The thing which is fundamentally and really frivolous is a careless solemnity....

To sum up the whole matter very simply, if Mr. McCabe asks me why I import frivolity into discussion of the nature of man, I answer, because frivolity is a part of the nature of man.

If he asks me why I introduce what he call paradoxes into a philosophical problem, I answer, because all philosophical problems tend to become paradoxical.

If he objects to my treating of life riotously, I reply that life is a riot.

And I say that the Universe as I see it, at any rate, is very much more like the fireworks at the Crystal Palace than it is like his own philosophy.

About the whole cosmos there is a tense and secret festivity-like preparations for Guy Fawkes day.

Eternity is the eve of something.

I never look up at the stars without feeling that they are the fires of a schoolboy's rocket, fixed in their everlasting fall.

Mr. McCabe: Joseph McCabe (1867–1955), a Roman Catholic priest turned rationalist; he left the priesthood in 1896 to begin a campaign against Christianity; his *Twelve Years in a Monastery* and

Modern Rationalism were published in 1897. *Crystal Palace:* giant glass-and-iron exhibition hall in London. *Guy Fawkes Day:* November 5, the day on which fireworks, masked children, and the burning of little effigies celebrate the arrest and execution of Guy Fawkes, who planned to blow up the Parliament building in 1605. *Source:* Excerpt from "Mr. McCabe and a Divine Frivolity," chapter 16 of *Heretics;* as it appears in CW1, 157–66.

5

HABITS OF DISCERNMENT

THE RASH VOWER

Paradoxy: Vows that aren't rash are no vows at all. *Hilarity:* Vows that produce a rash aren't much better. *Humility:* Vows are choices lovers make. *Scripture:* "Vow yourselves and all of your crowd to the Lord your God; and avow the vows as offerings to the *Deus Terribilis*" (Psalm VUL 75:12; NRSV 76:11)

If a prosperous Modern Man with a high hat and a frock coat were to solemnly pledge himself before all his clerks and friends to count the leaves on every third tree in Holland Walk, to hop up to the City on one leg every Thursday, to repeat the whole of Mill's *Liberty* seventy-six times, to collect 300 dandelions in fields belonging to anyone of the name of Brown, to remain for thirty-one hours holding his left ear in his right hand, to sing the names of all his aunts in order of age on the top of an omnibus, or make any such unusual undertaking, we should immediately conclude that the man was mad or, as it is sometimes expressed, was an artist in life.

Yet these vows are not more extraordinary than the vows which in the Middle Ages and in similar periods were made, not by fanatics merely, but by the greatest figures in civic and national civilization — by kings, judges, poets, and priests. One man swore to chain two mountains together, and the great chain hung there, it was said, for ages as a monument of that mystical folly. Another swore that he would find his way to Jerusalem with a patch over his eyes, and died looking for it.

It is not easy to see that these two exploits, judged from a strictly rational standpoint, are any saner than the acts above suggested. A mountain is commonly a stationary and reliable object which it is not necessary to chain up at night like a dog. And it is not easy at first sight to see that a man pays a very high compliment to the Holy City by setting out for it under conditions which render it to the last degree improbable that he will ever get there.

But about this there is one striking thing to be noticed. If men behaved in that way in our time, we should, as we have said, regard them as symbols of the *Decadence*. But the men who did these things were not decadent; they belonged generally to the most robust classes of what is generally regarded as a robust age. Again, it will be urged that if men essentially sane performed such insanities, it was under the capricious direction of a superstitious religious system. This, again, will not hold water; for in the purely terrestrial and even sensual departments of life, such as love and lust, the medieval princes show the same mad promises and performances, the same misshapen imagination, and the same monstrous self-sacrifice.

Here we have a contradiction, to explain which it is necessary to think of the whole nature of vows from the beginning. And if we consider seriously and correctly the nature of vows, we shall, unless I am much mistaken, come to the conclusion that it is perfectly sane, and even sensible, to swear to chain mountains together and that, if insanity is involved at all, it is a little insane not to do so.

The man who makes a vow makes an appointment with himself at some distant time or place. The danger of it is that he himself should not keep the appointment. And in modern times this terror of one's self, of the weakness and mutability of one's self, has perilously increased and is the real basis of the objection to vows of any kind. A Modern Man refrains from swearing to count the leaves on every third tree in Holland Walk, not because it is silly to do so (he does many sillier things), but because he has a profound conviction that before he had got to the three hundred and seventy-ninth leaf on the first tree, he would be excessively tired of the subject and want to go home to tea. In other words, we fear that by that time he will be, in the common but hideously significant phrase, "another man."

Now, it is this horrible Fairy Tale of a man constantly changing into other men that is the soul of the Decadence. That John Paterson should, with apparent calm, look forward to being a certain General Barker on Monday, Dr. Macgregor on Tuesday, Sir Walter Carstairs on Wednesday, and Sam Slugg on Thursday, may seem a nightmare; but to that nightmare we give the name of Modern Culture.

One great Decadent, who is now dead, published a poem some time ago in which he powerfully summed up the whole spirit of the movement by declaring that he could stand in the prison yard and entirely comprehend the feelings of a man about to be hanged.

> For he that lives more lives than one
> More deaths than one must die.

And the end of all this is that maddening horror of unreality which descends upon the Decadents, and compared with which physical pain itself would have the freshness of a youthful thing. The one Hell which imagination must conceive as most hellish is to be eternally acting a play without even the narrowest and dirtiest greenroom in which to be human. And this is the condition of the Decadent, of the Aesthete, of the Free-lover. To be everlastingly passing through dangers which we know cannot scare us, to be taking oaths which we know cannot bind us, to be defying enemies who we know cannot conquer us — this is the grinning tyranny of Decadence which is called freedom.

Let us turn, on the other hand, to the Maker of Vows. The man who made a vow, however wild, gave a healthy and natural expression to the greatness of a great moment. He vowed, for example, to chain two mountains together, perhaps a symbol of some great relief of love, or aspiration. Short as the moment of his resolve might be, it was, like all great moments, a moment of immortality, and the desire to say of it *exegi monumentum aere perennius* was the only sentiment that would satisfy his mind.

The modern Aesthetic Man would, of course, easily see the emotional opportunity; he would vow to chain two mountains together. But, then, he would quite as cheerfully vow to chain the earth to the moon. And the withering consciousness that he did not mean what he said; that he was, in truth, saying nothing of any great import, would take from him exactly that sense of daring actuality which is the excitement of a vow.

The revolt against vows has been carried in our day even to the extent of a revolt against the typical vow of marriage. It is most amusing to listen to the opponents of marriage on this subject. They appear to imagine that the ideal of constancy was a yoke mysteriously imposed on mankind by the Devil, instead of being, as it is, a yoke consistently imposed by all lovers on themselves.

They have invented a phrase, a phrase that is a black and white contradiction in two words — *free love* — as if a lover ever had been, or ever could be, free. It is the nature of love to bind itself, and the institution of marriage merely paid the average man the compliment of taking him at his word. Modern sages offer to the lover, with an ill-favored grin, the largest liberties and the fullest irresponsibility; but they do not respect him as the old Church respected him; they do not write his oath upon the heavens as the record of his highest moment. They give him every liberty except the liberty to sell his liberty, which is the only one that he wants.

It is exactly this backdoor, this sense of having a retreat be-hind us, that is, to our minds, the sterilizing spirit in modern pleasure. Everywhere there is the persistent and insane attempt to obtain pleasure without paying for it.

Thus, in politics the modern Jingoes practically say, "Let us have the pleasure of conquerors without the pains of soldiers: let us sit on sofas and be a hardy race."

Thus, in religion and morals, the Decadent Mystics say: "Let us have the fragrance of sacred purity without the sorrows of self-restraint; let us sing hymns alternately to the Virgin and Priapus."

Thus in love the Free-lovers say, "Let us have the splendor of offering ourselves without the peril of committing ourselves; let us see whether one cannot commit suicide an unlimited number of times."

Emphatically, it will not work. There are thrilling moments, doubtless, for the Spectator, the Amateur, and the Aesthete; but there is one thrill that is known only to the Soldier who fights for his own flag, to the Aesthetic who starves himself for his own illumination, to the Lover who makes finally his own choice.

And it is this transfiguring self-discipline that makes the vow a truly sane thing. It must have satisfied even the giant hunger of the soul of a lover or a poet to know that in consequence of some one instant of decision that strange chain would hang for centuries in the Alps among the silences of stars and snows. All around us is the City of Small Sins, abounding in backways and retreats, but surely, sooner or later, the towering flame will rise from the harbor announcing that the reign of the cowards is over and a man is burning his ships.

The Decadence: casual grouping of French and English poets at the turn of the twentieth century who wanted to free literature from commerce and industry and traditional morality. *Mill's Liberty:* John Stuart Mill (1806–1873), English philosopher and economist, au-thor of, among other influential books, *On Liberty* (1859). *Green*

room: backstage theater space where actors wait for their cues.
Exegi monumentum aere perennius: Latin for "I've built a monument more lasting than brass"; first line of an ode (Book 3, Ode
30) by Horace (65–8 B.C.E.), a poet the Emperor Caesar Augustus
felt he could call on from time to time for a rousing civic hymn.
Jingoes: advocates of a bellicose foreign policy; loud, blustering pa-
triots; supporters of sending the British fleet into Turkish waters to
resist Russia in 1878. *Priapus:* Greek and Roman God of procre-
ation whose symbol was Penis Bold Extended. *Source:* An abridged
version of a chapter in Chesterton's book *The Defendant.*

THE UNSUCCESSFUL MILLIONAIRE

Paradoxy: Money and the influence it can buy may be the key to
worldly success, but it's not the key to other-worldly success. *Hilarity:* Books on success aren't worth the money that's paid for them.
Humility: Success feeds on Avarice and Pride; Virtue feeds upon Simplicity. *Scripture:* "Rich and successful you may be, but now that
you're dead, only misery rains upon you. Your wealth offends your
nose, and your clothing makes meals for moths. Gold and silver you
may have, but they're turning to rust. It's the rust on your fingers
that'll give you away to the Final Judge, and your flesh will feel the
Final Fire. What about all those precious stones and metals you'd
been stashing away for your retirement? Well, I hate to tell you, but
they've all turned to Final Wrath" (James 5:1–3).

There has appeared in our time a particular class of books and
articles which I sincerely and solemnly think may be called the
silliest ever known among men. They are much more wild than
the wildest romances of chivalry and much more dull than the
dullest religious tract. Moreover, the romances of chivalry were
at least about chivalry; the religious tracts are about religion.

But these things are about nothing; they are about what is
called *Success.* On every bookstall, in every magazine, you may
find works telling people how to succeed. They are books showing men how to succeed in everything; they are written by men
who cannot even succeed in writing books.

To begin with, of course, there is no such thing as *Success*. Or, if you like to put it so, there is nothing that is not successful. That a thing is successful merely means that it is; a millionaire is successful in being a millionaire and a donkey in being a donkey. Any live man has succeeded in living; any dead man may have succeeded in committing suicide. But, passing over the bad logic and bad philosophy in the phrase, we may take it, as these writers do, in the ordinary sense of success in obtaining money or worldly position.

These writers profess to tell the Ordinary Man how he may succeed in his trade or speculation — how, if he is a builder, he may succeed as a builder; how, if he is a stockbroker, he may succeed as a stockbroker. They profess to show him how, if he is a grocer, he may become a sporting yachtsman; how, if he is a tenth-rate journalist, he may become a peer; and how, if he is a German Jew, he may become an Anglo-Saxon.

This is a definite and business-like proposal, and I really think that the people who buy these books — if any people do buy them — have a moral, if not a legal, right to ask for their money back. Nobody would dare to publish a book about electricity which literally told one nothing about electricity. No one would dare publish an article on botany which showed that the writer did not know which end of a plant grew in the earth. Yet our modern world is full of books about *Success* and successful people which literally contain no kind of idea and scarcely any kind of verbal sense.

It is perfectly obvious that in any decent occupation — such as bricklaying or writing books — there are only two ways, in any special sense, of succeeding. One is by doing very good work, the other is by cheating. Both are much too simple to require any literary explanation. If you are in for the high jump, either jump higher than anyone else, or manage somehow to pretend that you have done so. If you want to succeed at whist, either be a good whist player or play with marked cards. You may want a book about jumping; you may want a book about whist; you may want a book about cheating at whist. But you cannot want a book about *Success*.

Especially you cannot want a book about *Success* such as those which you can now find scattered by the hundred about the book market. You may want to jump or to play cards; but you do not want to read wandering statements to the effect that jumping is jumping, or that games are won by winners. If these writers, for instance, said anything about success in jumping, it would be something like this.

"The jumper must have a clear aim before him. He must desire definitely to jump higher than the other men who are in for the same competition. He must let no feeble feelings of mercy (sneaked from the sickening Little Englanders and Pro-Boers) prevent him from trying to *do his best*. He must remember that a competition in jumping is distinctly competitive and that, as Darwin has gloriously demonstrated, THE WEAKEST GO TO THE WALL."

That is the kind of thing the book would say, and very useful it would be, no doubt, if read out in a low and tense voice to a young man just about to take the high jump. Or suppose that in the course of his intellectual rambles the philosopher of *Success* dropped upon our other case, that of playing cards, his bracing advice would run —

"In playing cards it is very necessary to avoid the mistake, commonly made by Maudlin Humanitarians and Free Traders, of permitting your opponent to win the game. You must have grit and snap and *go in to win*. The days of idealism and superstition are over. We live in a time of science and hard common sense, and it has now been definitely proved that in any game where two are playing IF ONE DOES NOT WIN, THE OTHER WILL."

It is all very stirring, of course, but I confess that if I were playing cards, I would rather have some decent little book which told me the rules of the game. Beyond the rules of the game it is all a question either of talent or dishonesty; and I will undertake to provide either one or the other — which, it is not for me to say.

Turning over a popular magazine, I find a queer and amusing example. There is an article called "The Instinct That Makes People Rich." It is decorated in front with a formidable portrait of Lord Rothschild. There are many definite methods, honest and dishonest, which make people rich; the only "instinct" I know of which does it is that instinct which theological Christianity crudely describes as "the sin of Avarice." That, however, is beside the present point. I wish to quote the following exquisite paragraphs as a piece of typical advice as to how to succeed. It is so practical; it leaves so little doubt about what should be our next step.

"The name of Vanderbilt is synonymous with wealth gained by modern enterprise. 'Cornelius,' the founder of the family, was the first of the great American magnates of commerce. He started as the son of a poor farmer; he ended as a millionaire twenty times over.

"He had the money-making instinct. He seized his opportunities, the opportunities that were given by the application of the steam engine to ocean traffic, and by the birth of railway locomotion in the wealthy but underdeveloped United States of America, and consequently he amassed an immense fortune.

"Now it is, of course, obvious that we cannot all follow exactly in the footsteps of this great railway monarch. The precise opportunities that fell to him do not occur to us. Circumstances have changed. But, although this is so, still, in our own sphere and in our own circumstances, we *can* follow his general methods; we *can* seize those opportunities that are given us, and give ourselves a very fair chance of attaining riches."

In such strange utterances we see quite clearly what is really at the bottom of all these articles and books. It is not mere business; it is not even mere cynicism. It is mysticism; the horrible Mysticism of Money. The writer of that passage did not really have the remotest notion of how Vanderbilt made his money, or of how anybody else is to make his. He does, indeed, conclude his remarks by advocating some scheme, but it has nothing in the world to do with Vanderbilt. He merely wished to prostrate himself before the mystery of a millionaire.

For when we really worship anything, we love not only its clearness but its obscurity. We exult in its very invisibility. Thus, for instance, when a man is in love with a woman, he takes special pleasure in the fact that a woman is unreasonable. Thus, again, the very pious poet, celebrating his Creator, takes pleasure in saying that God moves in a mysterious way.

Now, the writer of the paragraphs which I have quoted does not seem to have had anything to do with a god, and I should not think, judging by his extreme unpracticality, that he had ever been really in love with a woman. But the thing he does worship — Vanderbilt — he treats in exactly this mystical manner. He really revels in the fact his deity Vanderbilt is keeping a secret from him. And it fills his soul with a sort of transport of cunning, an ecstasy of priestcraft, that he should pretend to be telling to the multitude that terrible secret which he does not know.

Speaking about the instinct that makes people rich, the same writer remarks —

"In the olden days its existence was fully understood. The Greeks enshrined it in the story of Midas, of the 'Golden Touch.' Here was a man who turned everything he laid his hands upon into gold. His life was a progress amidst riches. Out of everything that came in his way he created the precious metal. 'A foolish legend,' said the wiseacres of the Victorian age. 'A truth,' say we of today. We all know of such men. We are ever meeting or reading about such persons who turn everything they touch into gold. Success dogs their very footsteps. Their life's pathway leads unerringly upward. They cannot fail."

Unfortunately, however, Midas could fail; he did. His path did not lead unerringly upward. He starved because whenever he touched a biscuit or a ham sandwich, it turned to gold.

That was the whole point of the story, though the writer has to suppress it delicately, writing so near to a portrait of Lord Rothschild.

The old fables of mankind are, indeed, unfathomably wise, but we must not have them expurgated in the interests of Mr. Vanderbilt. We must not have King Midas represented as an example of success; he was a failure of an unusually painful kind. Also, he had the ears of an ass. Also (like most other prominent and wealthy persons) he endeavored to conceal the fact. It was his barber (if I remember right) who had to be treated on a confidential footing with regard to this peculiarity. And his barber, instead of behaving like a go-ahead person of the Succeed-at-all-costs school and trying to blackmail King Midas, went away and whispered this splendid piece of society scandal to the reeds, who enjoyed it enormously. It is said that they also whispered it as the winds swayed them to and fro.

I look reverently at the portrait of Lord Rothschild; I read reverently about the exploits of Mr. Vanderbilt. I know that I cannot turn everything I touch to gold. But then I also know that I have never tried, having a preference for other substances such as grass and good wine. I know that these people have certainly succeeded in something; that they have certainly overcome somebody; I know that they are kings in a sense that no men were ever kings before; that they create markets and bestride continents. Yet it always seems to me that there is some small domestic fact that they are hiding, and I have sometimes thought I heard upon the wind the laughter and whisper of the reeds.

At least, let us hope that we shall all live to see these absurd books about *Success* covered with a proper derision and neglect. They do not teach people to be successful, but they do teach people to be snobbish; they do spread a sort of evil poetry of worldliness.

The Puritans are always denouncing books that inflame Lust; what shall we say of books that inflame the viler passions of Avarice and Pride?

A hundred years ago we had the ideal of the Industrious Apprentice; boys were told that by thrift and work they would all become Lord Mayors. This was fallacious, but it was manly and had a minimum of moral truth.

In our society, Temperance will not help a poor man to enrich himself, but it may help him to respect himself. Good Work will not make him a rich man, but Good Work may make him a good workman.

The Industrious Apprentice rose by virtues few and narrow indeed, but still virtues. But what shall we say of the gospel preached to the new Industrious Apprentice — the Apprentice who rises not by his virtues, but avowedly by his vices?

Little Englanders: politicians and political theorists, most prominent from 1840 to 1870, who thought a Little England preferable to a vast Victorian Empire. *Pro-Boers:* supporters of Boer expansionism against indigenous South African peoples; England and the several Boer republics warred in 1880–81 and 1899–1902. *Darwin:* reference to Darwin's theory, expressed in his masterwork *On the Origin of Species* (1859), that in the evolutionary process the fittest survive, the flabbiest succumb. *Go to the wall:* are defeated or pushed aside. *Vanderbilt:* Cornelius Vanderbilt (1794–1877), American shipping and railroad magnate, who acquired a personal fortune of $100 million. *Source:* Excerpted from *All Things Considered* by G. K. Chesterton, from an edition by John Lane Company, New York, 1909.

THE UNSCIENTIFIC SCIENTIST

Paradoxy: The Scientist studies nature but, alas, not human nature. *Hilarity:* Science can analyze a pork chop, but not man's desire for, or abhorrence of, that pork chop. *Humility:* Man in all his humility should be the only subject of science. *Scripture:* "There are never enough studies, and never enough time for study" (Ecclesiastes 12:12).

A permanent disadvantage of the study of folklore and kindred subjects is that the man of science can hardly be, in the nature of things, very frequently a man of the world. He is a student of nature; he is scarcely ever a student of human nature. And even where this difficulty is overcome, and he is in some sense a student of human nature, this is only a very faint beginning of the painful progress toward being human.

For the study of primitive race and religion stands apart in one important respect from all, or nearly all, the ordinary scientific studies. A man can understand astronomy only by being an astronomer; he can understand entomology only by being an entomologist (or perhaps an insect); but he can understand a great deal of anthropology merely by being a man. He is himself the animal which he studies.

Hence arises the fact which strikes the eye everywhere in the records of ethnology and folklore — the fact that the same frigid and detached spirit which leads to success in the study of astronomy or botany leads to disaster in the study of mythology or human origins. It is necessary to cease to be a man in order to do justice to a microbe; it is not necessary to cease to be a man in order to do justice to men.

That same suppression of sympathies, that same waving away of intuitions or guesswork which make a man preternaturally clever in dealing with the stomach of a spider, will make him preternaturally stupid in dealing with the heart of man. He is making himself inhuman in order to understand humanity. An ignorance of the other world is boasted by many men of science; but in this matter their defect arises, not from ignorance of the other world, but from ignorance of this world.

For the secrets about which anthropologists concern themselves can be best learned, not from books or voyages, but from the ordinary commerce of man with man.

The secret of why some savage tribe worships monkeys or the moon is not to be found even by traveling among those savages and taking down their answers in a notebook, although the cleverest man may pursue this course. The answer to the riddle is in England; it is in London; nay, it is in his own heart.

When a man has discovered why men in Bond Street wear black hats, he will at the same moment have discovered why men in Timbuctoo wear red feathers.

The mystery in the heart of some savage war dance should not be studied in books of scientific travel; it should be studied at a subscription ball.

If a man desires to find out the origins of religions, let him not go to the Sandwich Islands; let him go to church.

If a man wishes to know the origin of human society, to know what society, philosophically speaking, really is, let him not go into the British Museum; let him go into society.

This total misunderstanding of the real nature of ceremonial gives rise to the most awkward and dehumanized versions of the conduct of men in rude lands or ages. The man of science, not realizing that ceremonial is essentially a thing which is done without a reason, has to find a reason for every sort of ceremonial and, as might be supposed, the reason is generally a very absurd one — absurd because it originates not in the simple mind of the barbarian, but in the sophisticated mind of the professor.

The learned man will say, for instance, "The natives of Mumbo-Jumbo Land believe that the dead man can eat, and will require food upon his journey to the other world. This is attested by the fact that they place food in the grave, and that any family not complying with this rite is the object of the anger of the priests and the tribe."

To anyone acquainted with humanity this way of talking is topsy-turvy. It is like saying, "The English in the twentieth century believed that a dead man could smell. This as attested by the fact that they always covered his grave with lilies, violets, or other flowers. Some priestly and tribal terrors were evidently attached to the neglect of this action, as we have records of several old ladies who were very much disturbed in mind because their wreaths had not arrived in time for the funeral."

It may be, of course that savages put food with a dead man because they think that a dead man can eat, or weapons with a dead man because they think that a dead man can fight. But, personally, I do not believe that they think anything of the kind. I believe they put food or weapons on the dead for the same reason that we put flowers, because it is an exceedingly natural and obvious thing to do. We do not understand, it is true, the emotion which makes us think it obvious and natural; but that is because, like all the important emotions of human existence, it is essentially irrational. We do not understand the savage for the same reason that the savage does not understand himself. And the savage does not understand himself for the same reason that we do not understand ourselves either.

The obvious truth is that the moment any matter has passed through the human mind, it is finally and for ever spoiled for all purposes of science. It has become a thing incurably mysterious and infinite; this mortal has put on immortality. Even what we call our material desires are spiritual, because they are human.

Science can analyze a pork chop, and say how much of it is phosphorus and how much is protein; but science cannot analyze any man's wish for a pork chop, and say how much of it is hunger, how much custom, how much nervous fancy, how much a haunting love of the beautiful. The man's desire for the pork chop remains literally as mystical and ethereal as his desire for Heaven.

All attempts, therefore, at a science of any human things, at a science of history, a science of folklore, a science of sociology, are by their nature not merely hopeless but crazy. You can no more be certain in economic history that a man's desire for money was merely a desire for money than you can be certain in hagiology that a saint's desire for God was merely a desire for God. And this kind of vagueness in the primary phenomena of the study is an absolutely final blow to anything in the nature of a science.

Timbuctoo: town on the edge of the Sahara; any extremely distant or remote place. *Subscription ball:* ball for a charitable cause.
Mumbo-Jumbo: grotesque idol or masked figure said to have been
worshiped among Mandingo peoples of western Africa. *Source:* Excerpt from chapter 11, "Science and the Savages," *Heretics;* as it
appears in cw1, 115–17.

THE IMPATIENT PATIENT

Paradoxy: The specific points of the argument may be fuzzy, but the
general drift is apparent. *Hilarity:* "He must not lie still if he wants
to be cured of a sin; on the contrary, he must get up and jump about
violently." *Humility:* Impatience is a virtue when it comes to throw-
ing off sin. *Scripture:* " 'Get up! Yes, you heard me. Stand up! It's
okay. You're standing all by yourself now. Yes, you can go home.'
So, right there in front of everybody, he got up, the first time in
many years, gathered up his belongings, and happily headed home.
'And your sins? I've taken care of them too' " (Matthew 9:6–7;
Mark 2:9, 11; John 5:11–12).

All Christianity concentrates on the man at the crossroads. The
vast and shallow philosophies, the huge syntheses of humbug,
all talk about ages and evolution and ultimate developments.
The true philosophy is concerned with the instant. Will a man
take this road or that? — That is the only thing to think about,
if you enjoy thinking.

The eons are easy enough to think about; anyone can think
about them. The instant is really awful; and it is because our
religion has intensely felt the instant that it has in Literature
dealt much with battle and in Theology dealt much with Hell.
It is full of danger, like a boy's book; it is at an immortal crisis.

There is a great deal of real similarity between popular fiction
and the religion of the western people. If you say that popular fiction is vulgar and tawdry, you only say what the dreary
and well-informed say also about the images in the Catholic
churches.

Life (according to the faith) is very like a serial story in a magazine. Life ends with the promise (or menace) "to be continued in our next." Also, with a noble vulgarity, life imitates the serial and leaves off at the exciting moment. For death is distinctly an exciting moment.

But the point is that a story is exciting because it has in it so strong an element of will, of what Theology calls Free Will. You cannot finish a sum how you like. But you can finish a story how you like. When somebody discovered the Differential Calculus, there was only one Differential Calculus he could discover. But when Shakespeare killed Romeo, he might have married him to Juliet's old nurse, if he had felt inclined. And Christendom has excelled in the narrative romance exactly because it has insisted on the theological free will.

It is a large matter and too much to one side of the road to be discussed adequately here; but this is the real objection to that torrent of modern talk about treating crime as disease, about making a prison merely a hygienic environment like a hospital, of healing sin by slow scientific methods.

The fallacy of the whole thing is that evil is a matter of active choice whereas disease is not. If you say that you are going to cure a profligate as you cure an asthmatic, my cheap and obvious answer is, "Produce the people who want to be asthmatics as many people want to be profligates." A man may lie still and be cured of a malady. But he must not lie still if he wants to be cured of a sin; on the contrary, he must get up and jump about violently.

The whole point indeed is perfectly expressed in the very word which we use for a man in hospital; "patient" is in the passive mood; "sinner" is in the active. If a man is to be saved from influenza, he may be a patient. But if he is to be saved from forging, he must be not a patient but an impatient. He must be personally impatient with forgery. All moral reform must start in the active not the passive will.

You cannot finish a sum how you like: This statement may be true
but, alas for Chesterton, it's not to say that 2 plus 3 always equals
5; it depends upon the base number of the mathematics. *Differential Calculus:* Alas for Chesterton, this branch of mathematics has
changed enough since 1702 to make it appear that there is indeed
more than one Differential Calculus. *Treating crime as disease:* Alas
for Chesterton, treating crime as disease has had at least one good
effect, that of not treating disease as crime; addiction is an instance.
Passive mood: Alas for Chesterton, in Latin the passive isn't a mood;
it's a voice; "patient" is derived from the indicative mood, present
participle active, of the verb "to suffer, undergo, feel pain, allow."
Perhaps Chesterton's confusion arose because *patior* is a deponent
verb; that's to say, passive in form but active in meaning, except for
the present participle, which is active in both form and meaning. *Active [mood]:* Alas for Chesterton, not mood, but voice. *In the active
not the passive will:* Alas for Chesterton, all acts of the will are, by
their very nature, active; those that seem passive are perhaps better described as permissive, if indeed they're acts of the will at all.
Source: Excerpt from "The Romance of Orthodoxy," chapter 8 of
Orthodoxy; as it appears in cw1, 329–45.

6

HABITS OF BELIEF

WHY I'M NOT A PAGAN

Paradoxy: "The New Paganism is no longer new, and it never at any time bore the smallest resemblance to [the Old] Paganism." *Hilarity:* "The term 'pagan' is continually used in fiction and light literature as meaning a man without any religion, whereas a pagan was generally a man with about half a dozen." *Humility:* "Pagans are depicted as, above all things, inebriate and lawless whereas they were, above all things, reasonable and respectable." *Scripture:* "The perennial virtues are Faith, Hope, and Charity — this I know, and this I know also — the greatest of these is Charity" (1 Corinthians 13:13).

The New Paganism is no longer new, and it never at any time bore the smallest resemblance to [the Old] Paganism. The ideas about the ancient civilization which it has left loose in the public mind are certainly extraordinary enough. The term "pagan" is continually used in fiction and light literature as meaning a man without any religion, whereas a pagan was generally a man with about half a dozen.

The pagans, according to this notion, were continually crowning themselves with flowers and dancing about in an irresponsible state whereas, if there were two things that the best pagan civilization did honestly believe in, they were a rather too rigid dignity and a much too rigid responsibility.

Pagans are depicted as above all things inebriate and lawless, whereas they were above all things reasonable and respectable.

They are praised as disobedient when they had only one great virtue — civic obedience. They are envied and admired as shamelessly happy when they had only one great sin — despair.

Mr. Lowes Dickinson, the most pregnant and provocative of recent writers on this and similar subjects, is far too solid a man to have fallen into this old error of the mere anarchy of Paganism. In order to make hay of that Hellenic enthusiasm which has as its ideal mere appetite and egotism, it is not necessary to know much Philosophy, but merely to know a little Greek. Mr. Lowes Dickinson knows a great deal of Philosophy, and also a great deal of Greek, and his error, if error he has, is not that of the crude hedonist. But the contrast which he offers between Christianity and Paganism in the matter of moral ideals — a contrast which he states very ably in a paper called "How long halt ye?" which appeared in the *Independent Review* — does, I think, contain an error of a deeper kind.

According to him, the ideal of Paganism was not, indeed, a mere frenzy of lust and liberty and caprice, but was an ideal of full and satisfied humanity. According to him, the ideal of Christianity was the ideal of asceticism.

When I say that I think this idea wholly wrong as a matter of Philosophy and History, I am not talking for the moment about any ideal Christianity of my own, or even of any primitive Christianity undefiled by after-events. I am not, like so many modern Christian idealists, basing my case upon certain things which Christ said. Neither am I, like so many other Christian idealists, basing my case upon certain things that Christ forgot to say.

I take historic Christianity with all its sins upon its head; I take it, as I would take Jacobinism, or Mormonism, or any other mixed or unpleasing human product, and I say that the meaning of its action was not to be found in asceticism.

I say that its point of departure from Paganism was not asceticism.

I say that its point of difference with the modern world was not asceticism. I say that St. Simeon Stylites had not his main inspiration in asceticism.

I say that the main Christian impulse cannot be described as asceticism, even in the ascetics.

Let me set about making the matter clear.

There is one broad fact about the relations of Christianity and Paganism which is so simple that many will smile at it, but which is so important that all moderns forget it. The primary fact about Christianity and Paganism is that one came after the other. Mr. Lowes Dickinson speaks of them as if they were parallel ideals — even speaks as if Paganism were the newer of the two, and the more fitted for a new age. He suggests that the pagan ideal will be the ultimate good of man. But if that is so, we must at least ask, with more curiosity than he allows for, why it was that man actually found his ultimate good on earth under the stars, and threw it away again. It is this extraordinary enigma to which I propose to attempt an answer.

There is only one thing in the modern world that has been face to face with Paganism; there is only one thing in the modern world which in that sense knows anything about Paganism: and that is Christianity. That fact is really the weak point in the whole of that hedonistic neo-Paganism of which I have spoken. All that genuinely remains of the ancient hymns or the ancient dances of Europe, all that has honestly come to us from the festivals of Phoebus or Pan, is to be found in the festivals of the Christian Church. If anyone wants to hold the end of a chain which really goes back to the heathen mysteries, he had better take hold of a festoon of flowers at Easter or a string of sausages at Christmas. Everything else in the modern world is of Christian origin, even everything that seems most anti-Christian.

The French Revolution is of Christian origin. The newspaper is of Christian origin. The anarchists are of Christian origin. Physical science is of Christian origin. The attack on Christianity is of Christian origin. There is one thing, and one thing only, in existence at the present day which can in any sense accurately be said to be of pagan origin, and that is Christianity.

The real difference between Paganism and Christianity is perfectly summed up in the difference between the pagan, or natural, virtues, and those three virtues of Christianity which the Church of Rome calls Virtues of Grace. The pagan, or rational, virtues are such things as Justice and Temperance, and Christianity has adopted them. The three mystical virtues which Christianity has not adopted but invented, are Faith, Hope, and Charity. Now much easy and foolish Christian rhetoric could easily be poured out upon those three words, but I desire to confine myself to the two facts which are evident about them.

The first evident fact (in marked contrast to the delusion of the dancing pagan) — the first evident fact, I say, is that the pagan virtues, such as Justice and Temperance, are the sad virtues, and that the mystical virtues of Faith, Hope, and Charity are the gay and exuberant virtues.

And the second evident fact, which is even more evident, is the fact that the pagan virtues are the reasonable virtues, and that the Christian virtues of Faith, Hope, and Charity are in their essence as unreasonable as they can be.

As the word "unreasonable" is open to misunderstanding, the matter may be more accurately put by saying that each one of these Christian or mystical virtues involves a paradox in its own nature, and that this is not true of any of the typically pagan or rationalist virtues.

Justice consists in finding out a certain thing due to a certain man and giving it to him. Temperance consists in finding out the proper limit of a particular indulgence and adhering to that. But Charity means pardoning what is unpardonable, or it is no virtue at all. Hope means hoping when things are hopeless, or it is no virtue at all. And Faith means believing the incredible, or it is no virtue at all.

It is somewhat amusing, indeed, to notice the difference between the fate of these three paradoxes in the fashion of the modern mind. Charity is a fashionable virtue in our time.... Hope is a fashionable virtue today.... But Faith is unfashionable, and it is customary on every side to cast against it the fact that it is a — paradox. Everybody mockingly repeats the famous childish definition that Faith is "the power of believing that which we know to be untrue." Yet it is not one atom more paradoxical than Hope or Charity.

Charity is the power of defending that which we know to be indefensible. Hope is the power of being cheerful in circumstances which we know to be desperate. It is true that there is a state of hope which belongs to bright prospects and the morning; but that is not the virtue of Hope. The virtue of Hope exists only in earthquake and eclipse. It is true that there is a thing crudely called Charity, which means Charity to the Deserving Poor; but Charity to the Deserving is not Charity at all, but Justice. It is the Undeserving who require it, and the ideal either does not exist at all, or exists wholly for them.

For practical purposes it is at the hopeless moment that we require the hopeful man, and the virtue either does not exist at all, or begins to exist at that moment. Exactly at the instant when Hope ceases to be reasonable, it begins to be useful....

Goldsworthy Lowes Dickinson: historian and man of letters (1862–1932) who wrote *The Greek View of Life* in 1896. *Jacobinism:* radical or revolutionary principles. *St. Simeon Stylites* (d. 459): an ascetic who spent the last thirty years of his life on top of a seventy-two-foot pillar, ably assisted by a rotating staff at the bottom. *Source:* Excerpt from "Paganism and Mr. Lowes Dickinson," chapter 12 of *Heretics,* CW1, 122–25.

WHY I'M A CHRISTIAN

Paradoxy: The perennial Christian loves both God and neighbor; the upstart Superman loves neither. *Hilarity:* "Anybody can define Conchology. Nobody can define Morals." *Humility:* "We've fallen with Adam, but we'll rise with Christ, not with the Superman." *Scripture:*

"How you have fallen from Heaven, Dawn-Breaker, Deal-Breaker, fallen to the earth in a heap for wreaking havoc among the nations!" (Isaiah 14:12).

I mean no disrespect to Mr. Blatchford in saying that our difficulty very largely lies in the fact that he, like masses of clever people nowadays, does not understand what Theology is. To make mistakes in a science is one thing, to mistake its nature another.

And as I read *God and My Neighbor,* the conviction gradually dawns on me that he thinks Theology is the study of whether a lot of tales about God told in the Bible are historically demonstrable. This is as if he were trying to prove to a man that Socialism was sound Political Economy, and began to realize halfway through that the man thought that Political Economy meant the study of whether politicians were economical.

It is very hard to explain briefly the nature of a whole living study; it would be just as hard to explain politics or ethics. For the more a thing is huge and obvious and stares one in the face, the harder it is to define. Anybody can define Conchology. Nobody can define Morals.

Nevertheless, it falls to us to make some attempt to explain this religious philosophy which was, and will be again, the study of the highest intellects and the foundation of the strongest nations, but which our little civilization has for a while forgotten, just as it has forgotten how to dance and how to dress itself decently.

I will try and explain why I think a religious philosophy necessary and why I think Christianity the best religious philosophy.

But before I do so I want you to bear in mind two historical facts. I do not ask you to draw my deduction from them or any deduction from them. I ask you to remember them as mere facts throughout the discussion.

1. Christianity arose and spread in a very cultured and very cynical world — in a very modern world. Lucretius was as much a materialist as Haeckel, and a much more persuasive writer. The Roman world had read *God and My Neighbor,* and in a weary sort of way thought it quite true. It is worth noting that religions almost always do arise out of these skeptical civilizations. A recent book on the Pre-Mohammedan literature of Arabia describes a life entirely polished and luxurious. It was so with Buddha, born in the purple of an ancient civilization. It was so with Puritanism in England and the Catholic Revival in France and Italy, both of which were born out of the rationalism of the Renaissance. It is so today; it is always so. Go to the two most modern and free-thinking centers, Paris and America, and you will find them full of devils and angels, of old mysteries and new prophets. Rationalism is fighting for its life against the young and vigorous superstitions.

2. Christianity, which is a very mystical religion, has nevertheless been the religion of the most practical section of mankind. It has far more paradoxes than the Eastern philosophies, but it also builds far better roads. The Moslem has a pure and logical conception of God, the one Monistic Allah. But he remains a barbarian in Europe, and the grass will not grow where he sets his foot. The Christian has a Triune God, "a tangled trinity," which seems a mere capricious contradiction in terms. But in action He bestrides the earth, and even the cleverest Eastern can only fight Him by imitating him first. The East has logic and lives on rice. Christendom has mysteries — and motor cars. Never mind, as I say, about the inference, let us register the fact.

Now with these two things in mind let me try and explain what Christian Theology is.

Complete Agnosticism is the obvious attitude for man. We are all Agnostics until we discover that Agnosticism will not work. Then we adopt some philosophy, Mr. Blatchford's or mine or some others, for of course Mr. Blatchford is no more an Agnostic than I am. The Agnostic would say that he did not know whether man was responsible for his sins. Mr. Blatchford says that he knows that man is not.

Here we have the seed of the whole huge tree of dogma. Why does Mr. Blatchford go beyond Agnosticism and assert that there is certainly no Free Will? *Because he cannot run his scheme of Morals without asserting that there is no Free Will.* He wishes no man to be blamed for sin. Therefore, he has to make his disciples quite certain that God did not make them free and therefore blamable. No wild Christian doubt must flit through the mind of the Determinist. No demon must whisper to him in some hour of anger that perhaps the company promoter was responsible for swindling him into the workhouse. No sudden skepticism must suggest to him that perhaps the schoolmaster was blamable for flogging a little boy to death.

The Determinist faith must be held firmly, or else certainly the weakness of human nature will lead men to be angered when they are slandered and kick back when they are kicked. In short, Free Will seems at first sight to belong to the Unknowable. Yet Mr. Blatchford cannot preach what seems to him common charity without asserting one dogma about it. And I cannot preach what seems to me common honesty without asserting another.

Here is the failure of Agnosticism. That our everyday view of the things we do (in the common sense) know, actually depends upon our view of the things we do not (in the common sense) know. It is all very well to tell a man, as the Agnostics do, to "cultivate his garden." But suppose a man ignores everything outside his garden, and among them ignores the sun and the rain?

This is the real fact. You cannot live without dogmas about these things. You cannot act for twenty-four hours without deciding either to hold people responsible or not to hold them responsible. Theology is a product far more practical than Chemistry.

Some Determinists fancy that Christianity invented a dogma like Free Will for fun — a mere contradiction. This is absurd. You have the contradiction whatever you are. Determinists tell me, with a degree of truth, that Determinism makes no difference to daily life. That means that although the Determinist knows men have no Free Will, yet he goes on treating them as if they had.

The difference then is very simple. The Christian puts the contradiction into his philosophy. The Determinist puts it into his daily habits. The Christian states as an avowed mystery what the Determinist calls nonsense. The Determinist has the same nonsense for breakfast, dinner, tea, and supper every day of his life.

The Christian, I repeat, puts the mystery into his philosophy. That mystery by its darkness enlightens all things. Once grant him that, and life is life, and bread is bread, and cheese is cheese; he can laugh and fight. The Determinist makes the matter of the will logical and lucid; and in the light of that lucidity all things are darkened, words have no meaning, actions no aim. He has made his philosophy a syllogism and himself a gibbering lunatic.

It is not a question between Mysticism and Rationality. It is a question between Mysticism and Madness. For Mysticism, and Mysticism alone, has kept men sane from the beginning of the world. All the straight roads of logic lead to some Bedlam, to Anarchism or to passive obedience, to treating the universe as a clockwork of matter or else as a delusion of mind. It is only the Mystic, the man who accepts the contradictions, who can laugh and walk easily through the world.

Are you surprised that the same civilization which believed in the Trinity discovered steam? All the great Christian doctrines are of this kind. Look at them carefully and fairly for yourselves.

I have only space for two examples.

The first is the Christian idea of God. Just as we have all been Agnostics, so we have all been Pantheists. In the godhood of youth it seems so easy to say, "Why cannot a man see God in a bird flying and be content?" But then comes a time when we go on and say, "If God is in the birds, let us be not only as beautiful as the birds; let us be as cruel as the birds; let us live the mad, red life of nature." And something that is wholesome in us resists and says, "My friend, you are going mad."

Then comes the other side and we say: "The birds are hateful, the flowers are shameful. I will give no praise to so base an universe." And the wholesome thing in us says: "My friend, you are going mad."

Then comes a fantastic thing and says to us: "You are right to enjoy the birds, but wicked to copy them. There is a good thing behind all these things, yet all these things are lower than you. The Universe is right: but the World is wicked. The thing behind all is not cruel, like a bird: but good, like a man." And the wholesome thing in us says. "I have found the high road."

Now when Christianity came, the ancient world had just reached this dilemma. It heard the Voice of Nature-Worship crying, "All natural things are good. War is as healthy as the flowers. Lust is as clean as the stars." And it heard also the cry of the hopeless Stoics and Idealists. "The flowers are at war. The stars are unclean. Nothing but man's conscience is right, and that is utterly defeated."

Both views were consistent, philosophical, and exalted. Their only disadvantage was that the first leads logically to murder, and the second to suicide. After an agony of thought the world saw the sane path between the two. It was the Christian God. He made Nature, but He was Man.

Lastly, there is a word to be said about the Fall. It can only be a word, and it is this. Without the doctrine of the Fall, all idea of progress is unmeaning. Mr. Blatchford says that there was not a Fall but a gradual rise. But the very word "rise" implies that you know toward what you are rising. Unless there is a standard you cannot tell whether you are rising or falling. But the main point is that the Fall, like every other large path of Christianity, is embodied in the common language talked on the top of an omnibus. Anybody might say, "Very few men are really manly." Nobody would say, "Very few whales are really whaley."

If you wanted to dissuade a man from drinking his tenth whisky, you would slap him on the back and say, "Be a man." No one who wished to dissuade a crocodile from eating his tenth explorer would slap it on the back and say, "Be a crocodile." For we have no notion of a perfect crocodile; no allegory of a whale expelled from his whaley Eden. If a whale came up to us and said, "I am a new kind of whale — I have abandoned whalebone," we should not trouble.

But if a man came up to us (as many will soon come up to us) to say, "I am a new kind of man, I am the Superman, I have abandoned mercy and justice," we should answer, "Doubtless you are new, but you are not nearer to the perfect man, for he has been already in the mind of God. We have fallen with Adam, and we shall rise with Christ. But we would rather fall with Satan than rise with you."

Mr. Blatchford: Robert Blatchford, editor of the *Clarion,* who wrote, over a period of two years, a series of articles attacking Christianity; GKC responded with three articles in 1904. *God and My Neighbor:* a rationalist credo by Blatchford and his friends. *Conchology:* branch of Zoology dealing with shells and shellfish. *Lucretius* (fl. first century B.C.E.): Latin poet and philosopher known for his long poem, *De rerum natura* (On the Nature of Things). *Haeckel:* Ernest Haeckel (1834–1919), German zoologist and evolutionist who out-Darwined Darwin. *Superman:* etymologically, a man of extraordinary power or ability; philosophically, an ideal

superior man of the future who'll justify the existence of the
human race; historically, the *Übermensch*, a sort of "Caesar with
Christ's soul" envisioned by nineteenth-century German philosopher
Friedrich Nietzsche; George Bernard Shaw translated the word as
"Superman" and wrote a play entitled *Man and Superman: A Comedy and a Philosophy,* a wildly successful production in London
at the time the "Blatchford Controversies" were being published
(1904). *Source:* "Why I'm a Christian," retitling of "Why I Believe
in Christianity," chapter 2 of *The Blatchford Controversies,* 1904;
as it appears in cw1, 381–85.

WHY I'M A CATHOLIC

Paradoxy: "Those who complain that Catholicism cannot say
anything new, seldom think it necessary to say anything new
about Catholicism." *Hilarity:* "Catholics have continually suffered
through supporting [new ideas] when they were really new; when
they were much too new to find any other support." *Humility:*
"The Catholic was not only first in the field but alone in the field;
and there was as yet nobody to understand what he had found
there." *Scripture:* "Warm your woolly selves by the fire and watch
your fleecy flocks. The Holy Spirit has made you bishops, shepherds
overseeing the church of God, something He paid dearly for with
His own blood" (Acts 20:28).

The difficulty of explaining "why I am a Catholic" is that there
are ten thousand reasons all amounting to one reason: that
Catholicism is true.

I could fill all my space with separate sentences each beginning with the words, "It is the only thing that. . . . " As, for
instance,

1. It is the only thing that really prevents a sin from being a
   secret.

2. It is the only thing in which the superior cannot be
   superior; in the sense of supercilious.

3. It is the only thing that frees a man from the degrading
   slavery of being a child of his age.

4. It is the only thing that talks as if it were the truth; as if it were a real messenger refusing to tamper with a real message.

5. It is the only type of Christianity that really contains every type of man; even the respectable man.

6. It is the only large attempt to change the world from the inside; working through wills and not laws; and so on.

Or I might treat the matter personally and describe my own conversion; but I happen to have a strong feeling that this method makes the business look much smaller than it really is. Numbers of much better men have been sincerely converted to much worse religions. I would much prefer to attempt to say here of the Catholic Church precisely the things that cannot be said even of its very respectable rivals.

In short, I would say chiefly of the Catholic Church that it is *catholic*. I would rather try to suggest that it is not only larger than me, but larger than anything in the world; that it is indeed larger than the world. But since in this short space I can only take a section, I will consider it in its capacity of a *Guardian of the Truth*.

The other day a well-known writer, otherwise quite well in-formed, said that the Catholic Church is always the enemy of new ideas. It probably did not occur to him that his own re-mark was not exactly in the nature of a new idea. It is one of the notions that Catholics have to be continually refuting be-cause it is such a very old idea. Indeed, those who complain that Catholicism cannot say anything new, seldom think it nec-essary to say anything new about Catholicism. As a matter of fact, a real study of history will show it to be curiously contrary to the fact.

In so far as the ideas really are ideas, and in so far as they can be new, Catholics have continually suffered through supporting them when they were really new; when they were much too new to find any other support. The Catholic was not only first in the field but alone in the field; and there was as yet nobody to understand what he had found there.

Thus, for instance, nearly two hundred years before the Declaration of Independence and the French Revolution, in an age devoted to the pride and praise of princes, Cardinal Bellarmine and Suarez the Spaniard laid down lucidly the whole theory of real Democracy. But in that age of Divine Right they only produced the impression of being sophistical and sanguinary Jesuits, creeping about with daggers to effect the murder of kings.

So, again, the Casuists of the Catholic schools said all that can really be said for the problem plays and problem novels of our own time, two hundred years before they were written. They said that there really are problems of moral conduct; but they had the misfortune to say it two hundred years too soon. In a time of tub-thumping fanaticism and free-and-easy vituperation, they merely got themselves called liars and shufflers for being psychologists before psychology was the fashion.

It would be easy to give any number of other examples down to the present day, and [to give] the case of ideas that are still too new to be understood.

There are passages in Pope Leo's *Encyclical on Labor* which are only now beginning to be used as hints for social movements much newer than socialism.

And when Mr. Belloc wrote about the *Servile State,* he advanced an economic theory so original that hardly anybody has yet realized what it is. A few centuries hence, other people will probably repeat it, and repeat it wrong. And then, if Catholics object, their protest will be easily explained by the well-known fact that Catholics never care for new ideas.

Nevertheless, the man who made that remark about Catholics meant something; and it is only fair to him to understand it rather more clearly than he stated it. What he meant was that, in the modern world, the Catholic Church is in fact the enemy of many influential fashions, most of which still claim to be new, though many of them are beginning to be a little stale.

In other words, in so far as he meant that the Church often attacks what the world at any given moment supports, he was perfectly right. The Church does often set herself against the fashion of this world that passes away; and she has experience enough to know how very rapidly it does pass away. But to understand exactly what is involved, it is necessary to take a rather larger view and consider the ultimate nature of the ideas in question, to consider, so to speak, *the idea of the idea.*

Nine out of ten of what we call new ideas are simply old mistakes. The Catholic Church has for one of her chief duties that of preventing people from making those old mistakes; from making them over and over again forever, as people always do if they are left to themselves.

The truth about the Catholic attitude toward heresy, or as some would say, toward liberty, can best be expressed perhaps by the metaphor of a map. The Catholic Church carries a sort of map of the mind which looks like the map of a maze, but which is in fact a guide to the maze. It has been compiled from knowledge which, even considered as human knowledge, is quite without any human parallel. There is no other case of one continuous intelligent institution that has been thinking about thinking for two thousand years. Its experience naturally covers nearly all experiences; and especially nearly all errors. The result is a map in which all the blind alleys and bad roads are clearly marked, all the ways that have been shown to be worthless by the best of all evidence: the evidence of those who have gone down them.

On this map of the mind the errors are marked as exceptions. The greater part of it consists of playgrounds and happy hunting fields, where the mind may have as much liberty as it likes; not to mention any number of intellectual battlefields in which the battle is indefinitely open and undecided. But it does definitely take the responsibility of marking certain roads as leading nowhere or leading to destruction, to a blank wall, or a sheer precipice. By this means, it does prevent men from wasting their time or losing their lives upon paths that have been found futile or disastrous again and again in the past, but which might otherwise entrap travelers again and again in the future. The Church does make herself responsible for warning her people against these; and upon these the real issue of the case depends. She does dogmatically defend humanity from its worst foes, those hoary and horrible and devouring monsters of the old mistakes.

Now all these false issues have a way of looking quite fresh, especially to a fresh generation. Their first statement always sounds harmless and plausible. I will give only two examples.

It sounds harmless to say, as most modern people have said: "Actions are only wrong if they are bad for society." Follow it out, and sooner or later you will have the inhumanity of a hive or a heathen city, establishing slavery as the cheapest and most certain means of production, torturing the slaves for evidence because the individual is nothing to the State, declaring that an innocent man must die for the people, as did the murderers of Christ. Then, perhaps, you will go back to Catholic definitions, and find that the Church, while she also says it is our duty to work for society, says other things also which forbid individual injustice.

Or again, it sounds quite pious to say, "Our moral conflict should end with a victory of the spiritual over the material." Follow it out, and you may end in the madness of the Manicheans, saying that a suicide is good because it is a sacrifice, that a sexual perversion is good because it produces no life, that the Devil made the sun and moon because they are material. Then you may begin to guess why Catholicism insists that there are evil spirits as well as good; and that materials also may be sacred, as in the Incarnation or the Mass, in the sacrament of marriage or the resurrection of the body.

Now there is no other corporate mind in the world that is thus on the watch to prevent minds from going wrong. The policeman comes too late when he tries to prevent men from going wrong. The doctor comes too late for he only comes to lock up a madman, not to advise a sane man on how not to go mad.

And all other sects and schools are inadequate for the purpose. This is not because each of them may not contain a truth, but precisely because each of them does contain a truth and is content to contain a truth. None of the others really pretends to contain the truth. None of the others, that is, really pretends to be looking out in all directions at once.

The Church is not merely armed against the heresies of the past or even of the present, but equally against those of the future that may be the exact opposite of those of the present. Catholicism is not ritualism; it may in the future be fighting some sort of superstitious and idolatrous exaggeration of ritual. Catholicism is not asceticism; it has again and again in the past repressed fanatical and cruel exaggerations of asceticism. Catholicism is not mere mysticism; it is even now defending human reason against the mere mysticism of the Pragmatists.

Thus, when the world went Puritan in the seventeenth century, the Church was charged with pushing charity to the point of sophistry, with making everything easy with the laxity of the confessional. Now that the world is not going Puritan but Pagan, it is the Church that is everywhere protesting against a Pagan laxity in dress or manners. It is doing what the Puritans wanted done when it is really wanted. In all probability, all that is best in Protestantism will only survive in Catholicism; and in that sense all Catholics will still be Puritans when all Puritans are Pagans.

Why I Am a Catholic: On July 30, 1922, Chesterton was welcomed into the Roman Catholic Church, not at the Benedictine Abbey at Douai, which would have been rather romantic, not to say swish, but at what would become his local church in Top Meadow,

Beaconsfield. Not a church really. Just a room in the Railway Ho-
tel. And that, a dance room "fitted up with Sir Philip Rose's chapel
fixtures" (MFF, 286). *Catholic Church . . . is Catholic:* "Catholic" because of its catholicity; traditionally, one of the four marks of the
Church — along with one, holy, and apostolic — since the second
century. *Guardian of the Truth:* no doubt an echo here of "Defender
of the Faith," the title Pope Leo X conferred in 1521 on Henry VIII,
later founder of the Anglican Church. *Cardinal Bellarmine:* Robert
Bellarmine (1542–1621): Italian Jesuit priest, theologian, eventual
cardinal who vigorously and eloquently opposed the Protestant doctrines of the Reformation; he was canonized in 1930. *Suarez the
Spaniard:* Francisco Suárez (1548–1617), Spanish Jesuit priest, theologian, and philosopher; a founder of international law. *Divine
Right:* the right deriving from the doctrine that kings have authority,
not from their subjects, but from God alone. *Sophistical and sanguinary Jesuits:* mythical Jesuits, as it turned out, who supposedly
roamed Europe as some sort of sacerdotal James Bond, confessors to
kings, advisers of prime ministers, educators of young nobles who'd
be the movers and shakers of the future; over the years the dar-
lings of second-rate novelists in whatever language. *Casuists of the
Catholic schools:* theologians who applied the principles of moral
theology and ethics to definite and concrete cases of human experience for the purpose of determining what one ought, or ought
not, to do. *Problem plays and problem novels:* nineteenth-century
plays no longer dealing with literary considerations but with such
topical but nonetheless perennial problems like prostitution, business ethics, illegitimacy, class structure; chief purveyors in the last
half of the nineteenth and first half of the twentieth centuries were
Norwegian Henrik Ibsen and his English translator, George Bernard
Shaw; the novel genre developed along the same line. *Encyclical
on Labor: Rerum Novarum:* encyclical of Pope Leo XIII (1891) on
the spirit of revolutionary change wrought by capital and labor on
the economies of the world. *Mr. Belloc:* "The fundamental position of *The Servile State* (1912) is this; that an Irish peasant who
earns almost no money but owns his own land, burns his own peat,
grows his own potatoes, and milks his own cow is a freer creature than a clerk or factory hand who might earn ten times more
money but is compelled to work for someone else and to live in
a rented or leased house and to be dependent on shopkeepers for
his sustenance" (ANW, 185). *Manicheans:* third-century religionists
whose doctrine was a cauldron of Christian and pagan ingredients,
celebrating Light battling Darkness and Satan as co-conspirator

with God. *Source:* Excerpt from "Why I Am a Catholic," a brief essay taken from the first edition of *Twelve Modern Apostles and Their Creed* (New York: Duffield and Company, 1926); as it appears in CW3, 127–32.

WHY I'M AN ELF

Paradoxy: The Nursery is the Church; the Nurse, "the solemn and star-appointed priestess"; Fairy Tales, the Revelation; Fairyland, "the sunny country of common sense"; the Elf, Chesterton himself, who in reality wasn't the mighty mite of Germanic mythology, but a full-bodied Tolkeinian figure that one wouldn't want to mess with in any century. *Hilarity:* "Old nurses do not tell children about the grass but about the Fairies that dance on the grass; and the old Greeks could not see the trees for the Dryads." *Humility:* "I am concerned with a certain way of looking at life, which was created in me by the Fairy Tales, but has since been meekly ratified by the mere facts." *Scripture:* "Father, Lord of Heaven and Earth," Jesus prayed. "At last I've got it. You're playing hide-and-seek with the Sage and the Prude, but You've spilled the beans to the Tots. Odd thing, this, but if it's what You want" (Matthew 11:25).

My first and last Philosophy, that which I believe in with unbroken certainty, I learned in the Nursery. I generally learned it from a Nurse; that is, from the solemn and star-appointed priestess at once of Democracy and Tradition.

The things I believed most then, the things I believe most now, are the things called *Fairy Tales*. They seem to me to be the entirely reasonable things. They are not fantasies: compared with them other things are fantastic. Compared with them Religion and Rationalism are both abnormal, though Religion is abnormally right and Rationalism abnormally wrong.

Fairyland is nothing but the sunny country of common sense. It is not Earth that judges Heaven, but Heaven that judges Earth. So for me at least it was not Earth that criticized Elfland, but Elfland that criticized the Earth. I knew the magic beanstalk before I had tasted beans; I was sure of the Man in the Moon before I was certain of the moon.

This was at one with all popular Tradition. Modern minor poets are naturalists, and talk about the bush or the brook; but the singers of the old epics and fables were supernaturalists, and talked about the gods of brook and bush. That is what the Moderns mean when they say that the Ancients did not "appreciate Nature," because they said that Nature was divine. Old Nurses do not tell children about the grass but about the Fairies that dance on the grass; and the old Greeks could not see the trees for the Dryads.

But I deal here with what Ethic and Philosophy come from being fed on Fairy Tales. If I were describing them in detail, I could note many noble and healthy principles that arise from them.

There is the chivalrous lesson of "Jack the Giant Killer," that giants should be killed because they are gigantic. It is a manly mutiny against Pride as such. For the rebel is older than all the kingdoms, and the Jacobin has more Tradition than the Jacobite.

There is the lesson of "Cinderella," which is the same as that of the Magnificat — *exaltavit humiles.*

There is the great lesson of "Beauty and the Beast," that a thing must be loved before it is loveable.

There is the terrible allegory of the "Sleeping Beauty," which tells how the human creature was blessed with all birthday gifts, yet cursed with death, and how death also may perhaps be softened to a sleep.

But I am not concerned with any of the separate statutes of Elfland, but with the whole Spirit of its Law, which I learned before I could speak, and shall retain when I cannot write.

I am concerned with a certain way of looking at life, which was created in me by the Fairy Tales, but has since been meekly ratified by the mere facts.

It might be stated this way.

There are certain sequences or developments (cases of one thing following another), which are, in the true sense of the word, reasonable. They are, in the true sense of the word, necessary. Such are mathematical and merely logical sequences. We in Fairyland, who are the most reasonable of all creatures, admit that reason and that necessity.

For instance, if the Ugly Sisters are older than Cinderella, it is, in an iron and awful sense, *necessary* that Cinderella is younger than the Ugly Sisters. There is no getting out of it. Haeckel may talk as much Fatalism about that fact as he pleases; it really must be.

If Jack is the son of a miller, a miller is the father of Jack. Cold Reason decrees it from her awful throne, and we in Fairyland submit.

If the Three Brothers all ride horses, there are six animals and eighteen legs involved: that is true rationalism, and Fairyland is full of it.

But as I put my head over the hedge of the Elves and began to take notice of the natural world, I observed an extraordinary thing. I observed that Learned Men in spectacles were talking of the actual things that happened — dawn and death and so on — as if *they* were rational and inevitable. They talked as if the fact that trees bear fruit were just as necessary as the fact that two and one trees make three. But it is not.

There is an enormous difference by the test of Fairyland, which is the test of the imagination. You cannot *imagine* two and one not making three. But you can easily imagine trees not growing fruit; you can imagine them growing golden candlesticks or tigers hanging on by the tail.

These men in spectacles spoke much of a man named Newton, who was hit by an apple, and who discovered a law. But they could not be got to see the distinction between a true law, a law of reason, and the mere fact of apples falling. If the apple hit Newton's nose, Newton's nose hit the apple. That is a true *necessary* because we cannot conceive the one occurring without the other.

But we can quite well conceive the apple not falling on his nose; we can fancy it flying ardently through the air to hit some other nose, of which it had a more definite dislike.

We have always in our Fairy Tales kept this sharp distinction between the Science of Mental Relations, in which there really are laws, and the Science of Physical Facts, in which there are no laws, but only weird repetitions. We believe in bodily miracles, but not in mental impossibilities. We believe that a Beanstalk climbed up to heaven, but that does not at all confuse our convictions on the philosophical question of how many beans make five.

Here is the peculiar perfection of tone and truth in the nursery tales. The Man of Science says, "Cut the stalk, and the apple will fall," but he says it calmly as if the one idea really led up to the other. The Witch in the Fairy Tale says, "Blow the horn, and the ogre's castle will fall," but she does not say it as if it were something in which the effect obviously arose out of the cause. Doubtless she has given the advice to many champions and has seen many castles fall, but she does not lose either her wonder or her reason. She does not muddle her head until it imagines a necessary mental connection between a horn and a falling tower.

But the Scientific Men do muddle their heads, until they imagine a necessary mental connection between an apple leaving the tree and an apple reaching the ground. They do really talk as if they had found not only a set of marvelous facts but a truth connecting those facts. They do talk as if the connection of two strange things physically connected them philosophically. They feel that because one incomprehensible thing constantly follows another incomprehensible thing the two together somehow make up a comprehensible thing. Two black riddles make a white answer.

In Fairyland we avoid the word "law," but in the Land Of Science they are singularly fond of it. Thus they will call some interesting conjuncture about how Forgotten Folks pronounced the alphabet, *Grimm's Law*. But Grimm's Law is far less intellectual than *Grimm's Fairy Tales*. The tales are, at any rate, certainly tales; while the law is not a law. A law implies that we know the nature of the generalization and enactment; not merely that we have noticed some of the effects.

If there is a law that pickpockets shall go to prison, it implies that there is an imaginable mental connection between the idea of prison and the idea of picking pockets. And we know what the idea is. We can say why we take liberty from a man who takes liberties. But we cannot say why an egg can turn into a chicken any more than we can say why a bear could turn into a Fairy Prince. As *ideas*, the egg and the chicken are further off from each other than the bear and the prince; for no egg in itself suggests a chicken, whereas some princes do suggest bears.

Granted, then, that certain transformations do happen, it is essential that we should regard them in the philosophic manner of Fairy Tales, not in the unphilosophic Science and the "Laws of Nature." When we are asked why eggs turn to birds or fruits fall in autumn, we must answer exactly as the Fairy Godmother would answer if Cinderella asked her why mice turned to horses or her clothes fell from her at twelve o'clock.

We must answer that it is *magic*. It is not a "law," for we do not understand its general formula. It is not a necessity, for though we can count on it happening practically, we have no right to say that it must always happen. It is no argument for unalterable law (as Huxley fancied) that we count on the ordinary course of things. We do not count on it; we bet on it. We risk the remote possibility of a miracle as we do that of a poisoned pancake or a world-destroying comet. We leave it out of account, not because it is a miracle, and therefore an impossibility, but because it is a miracle, and therefore an exception.

All the terms used in the science books, "law," "necessity," "order," "tendency," and so on, are really unintellectual because they assume an inner synthesis, which we do not possess. The only words that ever satisfied me as describing Nature are the terms used in the Fairy Books, "charm," "spell," "enchantment." They express the arbitrariness of the fact and its mystery. A tree grows fruit because it is a magic tree. Water runs downhill because it is bewitched. The sun shines because it is bewitched.

I deny altogether that this is fantastic or even mystical. We may have some mysticism later on; but this fairy-tale language about things is simply rational and agnostic. It is the only way I can express in words my clear and definite perception that one thing is quite distinct from another, that there is no logical connection between flying and laying eggs. It is the man who talks about "a law" that he has never seen who is the mystic.

Nay, the ordinary Scientific Man is strictly a Sentimentalist. He is a Sentimentalist in this essential sense, that he is soaked and swept away by mere associations. He has so often seen birds fly and lay eggs that he feels as if there must be some dreamy, tender connection between the two ideas, whereas there is none.

A Forlorn Lover might be unable to dissociate the moon from lost love; so the Materialist is unable to dissociate the moon from the tide. In both cases there is no connection, except that one has seen them together.

A Sentimentalist might shed tears at the smell of apple blossom because, by a dark association of his own, it reminded him of his boyhood.

So the Materialist Professor (though he conceals his tears) is yet a sentimentalist because, by a dark association of his own, apple blossoms remind him of apples.

But the Cool Rationalist from Fairyland does not see why, in the abstract, the apple tree should not grow crimson tulips; it sometimes does in his country.

This elementary wonder, however, is not a mere fancy derived from the Fairy Tales; on the contrary, all the fire of the Fairy Tales is derived from this. Just as we all like love tales because there is an instinct of sex, we all like astonishing tales because they touch the nerve of the ancient instinct of astonishment. This is proved by the fact that when we are very young children, we do not need Fairy Tales; we only need tales. Mere life is interesting enough.

A child of seven is excited by being told that Tommy opened a door and saw a dragon. But a child of three is excited by being told that Tommy opened a door. Boys like romantic tales, but babies like realistic tales because they find them romantic. In fact, a baby is about the only person, I should think, to whom a modern realistic novel could be read without boring him. This proves that even nursery tales only echo an almost prenatal leap of interest and amazement. These tales say that apples were golden only to refresh the forgotten moment when we found that they were green. They make rivers run with wine only to make us remember, for one wild moment, that they run with water.

I have said that this is wholly reasonable and even agnostic. And, indeed, on this point I am all for the Higher Agnosticism; its better name is Ignorance. We have all read in scientific books and, indeed, in all romances, the story of the man who has forgotten his name. This man walks about the streets and can see and appreciate everything; only he cannot remember who he is.

Well, Everyman is that man in the story. Everyman has forgotten who he is. One may understand the cosmos, but never the ego; the self is more distant than any star. *Thou shalt love the Lord thy God; but thou shalt not know thyself.*

We are all under the same mental calamity; we have all forgotten our names. We have all forgotten what we really are. All that we call Common Sense and Rationality and Practicality and Positivism only means that for certain dead levels of our life we forget that we have forgotten. All that we call Spirit and Art and Ecstasy only means that for one awful instant we remember that we forget.

But though, like the man without memory in the novel, we walk the streets with a sort of half-witted admiration, still it is admiration. It is admiration in English and not only admiration in Latin. The wonder has a positive element of praise....

Here I am only trying to describe the enormous emotions which cannot be described. And the strongest emotion was that life was as precious as it was puzzling. It was an ecstasy because it was an adventure; it was an adventure because it was an opportunity. The goodness of the Fairy Tale was not affected by the fact that there might be more dragons than princesses; it was good to be in a Fairy Tale.

The test of all happiness is gratitude, and I felt grateful, though I hardly knew to whom.

Children are grateful when Santa Claus puts in their stockings gifts of toys or sweets.

Could I not be grateful to Santa Claus when he put in my stockings the gift of two miraculous legs?

We thank people for birthday presents of cigars and slippers. Can I thank no one for the birthday present of birth?

Fairy Tales: tales in which Fairies and other rather marvelous creatures undergo one harum-scarum adventure after another; more than enough, if one took them seriously, to scare child or adult; chief English purveyor during Chesterton's sojourn in Elfland was Andrew Lang; he published twelve collections of stories, each with a color in the title, beginning with *The Blue Fairy Book* (1889) and ending with *The Lilac Fairy Book* (1910). *Elfland:* apparently, a land of Chesterton's own devising. *Dryads:* in Greek mythology, wood nymphs. *Jacobin:* political group in the French Revolution. *Jacobite:* Scottish supporter of the House of Stuart following the Revolution of 1688, when the last Stuart monarch, James II, was deposed. *Magnificat:* in the Latin Vulgate the first word of Mary's reply to the Angel who made the awful proposal; "My soul *magnifies* the Lord"; Luke 1:46–55. *Exaltavit humiles:* latter part of verse 52 of the *Magnificat;* "God has dumped the powerful from their thrones, and He has *exalted the humble.*" *Haeckel:* Ernest Haeckel (1834–1919), German zoologist and evolutionist who tried to out-Darwin Darwin. *Three Brothers:* characters in more than one Fairy Tale. *Two and one trees make three:* only in a base-10 mathematics; even in Chesterton's time mathematicians were already imagining an infinite number of other basimals, in most of which two and one wouldn't necessarily make three. *Newton:* Isaac Newton (1642/43–1727), English physicist and mathematician who, among other things, formulated the law of universal gravitation. *Grimm's Law:* a statement in historical linguistics to the effect that Indo-European languages have a number of consonantal sounds in common although they may be expressed by different consonantal letters or characters in each language; first noticed by Danish philologist Rasmus Kristian Rask in 1814 and popularized some decades later by German grammarian and philologist Jacob Grimm; happily remembered as one of the Brothers Grimm. *Grimm's Fairy Tales:* classic collection of folk tales by the Grimm brothers, Jacob (1785–1863) and Wilhelm (1786–1859). *Magic:* not Houdini prestidigitation, but human imagination. *Huxley:* Thomas H. Huxley (1825–95), English biologist whose speculations on philosophy and religion and whose promotion of Darwinism led him to agnosticism. *Source:* Excerpt from "The Ethics of Elfland," chapter 4 of *Orthodoxy,* 1908; as it appears in CW1, 249–68.

WHY I'M A CLOWN

Paradoxy: "To the Modern Man the heavens are actually below the earth. The explanation is simple; he is standing on his head, which is a very weak pedestal to stand on." *Hilarity:* "Pessimism is at best an emotional half-holiday; Joy is the uproarious labor by which all things live." *Humility:* "There was some one thing that was too great for God to show us when He walked upon our earth, and I have sometimes fancied that it was His mirth." *Scripture:* "You see all these people? They do stuff Caesar doesn't approve of, and they say things that'd make Caesar's eyes pop. Like they have another king. Who? Jesus!" (Acts 17:6).

The mass of men have been forced to be gay about the little things, but sad about the big ones. Nevertheless (I offer my last dogma defiantly), it is not native to man to be so. Man is more himself, man is more manlike, when Joy is the fundamental thing in him, and Grief the superficial. Melancholy should be an innocent interlude, a tender and fugitive frame of mind; Praise should be the permanent pulsation of the soul. Pessimism is at best an emotional half-holiday; Joy is the uproarious labor by which all things live. Yet, according to the apparent Estate of Man as seen by the Pagan or the Agnostic, this primary need of human nature can never be fulfilled. Joy ought to be expansive, but for the Agnostic it must be contracted; it must cling to one corner of the world. Grief ought to be a concentration; but for the Agnostic its desolation is spread through an unthinkable eternity.

This is what I call being born upside down. The Skeptic may truly be said to be topsy-turvy, for his feet are dancing upward in idle ecstasies while his brain is in the abyss. To the Modern Man the heavens are actually below the earth. The explanation is simple; he is standing on his head, which is a very weak pedestal to stand on. But when he has found his feet again, he knows it. Christianity satisfies suddenly and perfectly man's ancestral instinct for being the right way up; satisfies it supremely in this, that by its creed Joy becomes something gigantic, and Sadness something special and small.

The vault above us is not deaf because the universe is an idiot; the silence is not the heartless silence of an endless and aimless world. Rather the silence around us is a small and pitiful stillness like the prompt stillness in a sick room. We are perhaps permitted tragedy as a sort of merciful comedy, because the frantic energy of divine things would knock us down like a drunken farce. We can take our own tears more lightly than we could take the tremendous levities of the angels. So we sit perhaps in a starry chamber of silence while the laughter of the heavens is too loud for us to hear.

Joy, which was the small publicity of the Pagan, is the gigantic secret of the Christian. And as I close this chaotic volume, I open again the strange small book from which all Christianity came; and I am again haunted by a kind of confirmation.

The tremendous figure which fills the Gospels towers in this respect, as in every other, above all the thinkers who ever thought themselves tall.

His pathos was natural, almost casual. The Stoics, ancient and modern, were proud of concealing their tears. He never concealed His tears; He showed them plainly on His open face at any daily sight, such as the far sight of His native city. Yet He concealed something....

Solemn Supermen and Imperial Diplomatists are proud of restraining their anger. He never restrained His anger. He flung furniture down from the steps of the Temple and asked men how they expected to escape the damnation of Hell. Yet He restrained something....

I say it with reverence — there was in that shattering personality a thread that must be called shyness.

There was something that He hid from all men when He went up a mountain to pray.

There was something that He covered constantly by abrupt silence or impetuous isolation.

There was some one thing that was too great for God to show us when He walked upon our earth, and I have sometimes fancied that it was His mirth.

Chaotic volume: Orthodoxy; specifically the last chapter. *Strange small book:* the Bible. *Stoics:* members of an ancient Greek school of Philosophy (circa 300 B.C.E.), holding austere ethical doctrines. *Source:* Excerpt from "Authority and the Adventurer," chapter 9 of *Orthodoxy;* as it appears in cw1, 346–66.

7

HABITS OF DEBATE

"Do We Agree?" was a debate, billed by the BBC in 1927 as "The Great Debate," the classical confrontation of Christian ideas with the erroneous ideas of the age. It was a bruising affair, requiring virtually every Christian virtue imaginable, but especially those virtues or habits of the heart, mind, and soul, coupled with the full knowledge of the virtues or habits of Society and Church, that are found in this Anthology. In the transcript of the debate that follows, against his arch foe George Bernard Shaw, Chesterton gives as good as he gets and, in return from his admirable foe, he gets what he gave.

DO WE AGREE?

A debate between
G. K. CHESTERTON
&
G. B. SHAW
with
HILAIRE BELLOC
in the chair.

A PREFATORY NOTE

In justice to all concerned, I feel it to be my duty to state frankly that this account of a public discussion between Mr. Chesterton and Mr. Shaw is something less than a verbatim report. But with some assistance from the debaters, it has been possible to save enough from oblivion to justify publication.   — CECIL PALMER, London, 1928.

This debate, which took place in 1927 — either on the last Friday in October (MFF, 316) or in December (ASD, 265) — was sponsored by the newly formed Distributist League (1926), an activist organization whose prime goal was to distribute, or re-distribute, the wealth — or was it the power? — of England.

The topic for debate — or inquiry, as Chesterton called it — was "Whether men should be free to possess private means."

The locale was Kingsway Hall.

To broadcast it live, the British Broadcast Company paid a fee — perhaps as much as £100 — something unheard of for a debate, but then again they'd never broadcast a debate before, let alone a debate of two hours' length.

*Each debater would make three speeches: one of thirty min-
utes; one of fifteen minutes; one of ten minutes. The chair would
open and close the debate with as few remarks as possible.*

*Arguing for the Distributist League was Chesterton: once a
Socialist, once a Liberal, now a Distributist; but always a me-
dievalist, it seemed, but with the decidedly unmedieval point of
view that land should be distributed to all those who didn't
have it. "To give nearly everybody ordinary houses," wrote
Chesterton, "would please nearly everybody" (CW4, 74). "Every
man should have his own home" — that would have been the
motto if the League had one.*

*Invited to present the opposite point of view was the Fabian
Society, a socialist group founded in 1883–84, having as its goal
the establishment of a democratic socialist state in England.
Because of their influential but limited membership, evolution
rather than revolution was the strategy they agreed upon.*

*For such an aggregation the appropriate name had to be
"Fabian," after the Roman general Fabius, who earned the so-
briquet "Cunctator" (Procrastinator); that's to say, he made a
virtue out of a defect, avoiding pitched battles with stronger
forces while fretting away at their lines until they succumbed
to confusion and exhaustion.*

*Powerful spokesman for the Fabians, and indeed its repre-
sentative in this debate, was Shaw, the formidable Irish comic
dramatist who achieved fame on the London and world stages;
literary, dramatic, and music critic, essayist on a vast number of
serious contemporary issues. Inevitably, GBS found himself on
the other side of an argument, any argument, with GKC, whom
he valued as a faithful friend and foe.*

*"The hall was full, and a large crowd was gathered outside,"
or so wrote Shaw's biographer, Archibald Henderson. "Chesterton had not arrived. When Shaw walked in and mounted the
platform, he was greeted with resounding applause. He rose
from his seat and said, earnestly, 'I am sorry, but I am not
Mr. Chesterton' " (AH, 845).*

Chairing the debate was Hilaire Belloc (1870–1953); close friend of Chesterton's, friendly foe of Shaw's. He opened and closed the debate with nonsensical remarks and, during it, doodled a nonsensical poem on the debate topic, which he felt compelled to read at the end.

As air time approached, the doors were locked and the audience hushed. On cue Belloc began to speak. Some noise was noticed at the doors. Shaw was making his introductory remarks — something to the effect that he and Chesterton were "madmen," itinerant intellectuals who were expected to entertain an audience; if at the same time they informed the audience on an important social issue, so much the better — when the doors burst open and the late, but angry, ticket-holders poured in. Quiet restored, Shaw sailed smoothly on.

The transcript of the debate, revised by both Chesterton and Shaw, was put into book form in 1928 by Cecil Palmer, publisher of some of GKC's later works.

Some seventy-five years later, as we read the transcript, we find the debate topic even more pressing than then and, perhaps, even more entertaining.

"What larks!" we can cry with Dickens's Joe Gargery. "What larks!"

"The Great Debate" was a return match of one held in 1911 with the same three participants. What Shaw described in a letter dated October 27, 1911, still held true for 1927.

"The disadvantages for us [in following the rules agreed to by both parties] are that we both want Belloc to let himself go.... We shall all three talk all over the shop — possibly never reaching the Socialism department — and Belloc will not trouble himself about the rules of public meeting and debate, even if there were any reason to suppose that he is acquainted with them.... I therefore conclude that we had better make it to some extent a clowns' cricket match.... As this is going to be a performance in which three Macs who are on the friendliest

terms in private will belabor each other recklessly on wooden
scalps and pillowed waistcoats and trouser seats, we need not
be particular [about the rules]" (quoted in MW, 365–66).

In conclusion, it would be a serious mistake for the twenty-
first-century reader to think that this debate wasn't a serious
exercise, no matter how charming, even cunning, the debaters
may have seemed before it or during it. In England redistribu-
tion of the wealth was and continues to be a desperate social
justice issue.

> *Scripture:* "Don't fuss with your adversary. Do come to some sort of
> agreement with him. You don't want him to turn on you and hand
> your head to the judge. You know what that means. He won't let
> you go until you've given him every last penny, whether you owe
> it to him or not" (Matthew 5:25–26). *Scripture:* "Listen carefully.
> I'm going to tell you this only once. Whenever two people hammer
> out an agreement on earth, it'll be ratified by my Father in Heaven.
> How can this be? Well, whenever two or three of you debate about
> a subject that's dear to my heart, I'm right there in the thick of it"
> (Matthew 18:19–20). *Scripture:* "The kingdom of Heaven is like a
> local vineyard. Standard pay is a denarius a day, and it's good pay.
> Early in the morning migrant workers agree to the terms.... My
> friend, I do you no injury. Didn't you agree with me to work for
> a denarius? Take it, it's yours, and hit the road. What I mean to say
> is, don't I have the right to give the same pay to the last hired as to
> the first hired? So why are you giving me the evil eye when I've just
> done such a good thing? What's the moral? The last shall be first,
> and the first, last. Many are called to work as day laborers, but only
> a few are hired full time" (Matthew 20:1–16).

Mr. Belloc:

I am here to take the chair in the debate between two men
whom you desire to hear more than you could possibly desire
to hear me.

They will debate whether they agree or do not agree. From
what I know of attempts at agreement between human beings
there is a prospect of a very pretty fight.

When men debate agreement between nations, then you may be certain a disastrous war is on the horizon.

I make an exception for the League of Nations, of which I know nothing. If the League of Nations could make a war, it would be the only thing it ever has made.

I do not know what Mr. Chesterton is going to say. I do not know what Mr. Shaw is going to say. If I did, I would not say it for them.

I vaguely gather from what I have heard that they are going to try to discover a principle.

Whether men should be free to possess private means.

As is Mr. Shaw.

As is Mr. Chesterton.

Or should be, like myself, an embarrassed person, a publishers' hack.

I could tell them; but my mouth is shut.

I am not allowed to say what I think.

At any rate, they are going to debate this sort of thing.

I know not what more to say.

They are about to debate.

You are about to listen.

I am about to sneer.

Mr. Shaw:

Mr. Belloc, and Ladies and Gentlemen. Our subject this evening, *"Do We Agree?"* was an inspiration of Mr. Chesterton's. Some of you might reasonably wonder, if we agree, what we are going to debate about. But I suspect that you do not really care much what we debate about, provided we entertain you by talking in our characteristic manners.

The reason for this, though you may not know it — and it is my business to tell you — is that Mr. Chesterton and I are two madmen. Instead of doing honest and respectable work and behaving ourselves as ordinary citizens, we go about the world possessed by a strange gift of tongues — in my own case almost exclusively confined to the English language — uttering all sorts of extraordinary opinions for no reason whatever.

Mr. Chesterton tells and prints the most extravagant lies. He takes ordinary incidents of human life — commonplace middle-class life — and gives them a monstrous and strange and gigantic outline. He fills suburban gardens with the most impossible murders, and not only does he invent the murders but also succeeds in discovering the murderer who never committed the murders.

I do very much the same sort of thing. I promulgate lies in the shape of plays; but whereas Mr. Chesterton takes events which you think ordinary and makes them gigantic and colossal to reveal their essential miraculousness, I am rather inclined to take these things in their utter commonplaceness, and yet to introduce among them outrageous ideas which scandalize the ordinary playgoer and send him away wondering whether he has been standing on his head all his life or whether I am standing on mine.

A man goes to see one of my plays and sits by his wife. Some apparently ordinary thing is said on the stage, and his wife says to him, "Aha! What do you think of that?" Two minutes later another apparently ordinary thing is said, and the man turns to his wife and says to her, "Aha! What do you think of that?"

Curious, is it not, that we should go about doing these things and be tolerated and even largely admired for doing them? Of late years I might say that I have almost been reverenced for doing these things. Obviously we are mad; and in the East we should be reverenced as madmen. The wisdom of the East says "Let us listen to these men carefully, but let us not forget that they are madmen." In this country they say "Let us listen to these amusing chaps; they are perfectly sane, which we obviously are not."

Now there must be some reason for showing us all this consideration. There must be some force in nature which....

(At this point the debate was interrupted by persistent knocking at the doors by ticket-holders who had, through some misunderstanding, been locked out. On the chairman's intervention the doors were opened, and order was restored. Mr. Shaw then proceeded.)

Ladies and Gentlemen, I must go on because, as you see, if I don't begin to talk, everybody else does.

Now I was speaking of the curious respect in which mad people are held in the East and in this country. What I was leading up to is this, that it matters very little on what points they differ. They have all kinds of aberrations which rise out of their personal circumstances, out of their training, out of their knowledge or ignorance.

But if you listen to them carefully and find that at certain points they agree, then you have some reason for supposing that here the Spirit of the Age is coming through and giving you an inspired message. Reject all the contradictory things they say and concentrate your attention on the things upon which they agree, and you may be listening to the voice of revelation.

You will do well tonight to listen attentively because, probably, what is urging us to these utterances is not personal to ourselves but some conclusion to which all mankind is moving either by reason or by inspiration. The mere fact that Mr. Chesterton and I may agree upon any point may not at all prevent us from debating it passionately. I find that the people who fight me generally hold the very ideas I am trying to express. I do not know if it is because they resent the liberty I am taking or because they do not like the words I use or the twist of my mind, but they are the people who quarrel most with me.

You have at this moment a typical debate raging in the Press. You have a very pretty controversy going on in the Church of England between the Archbishop of Canterbury and the Bishop of Birmingham.

I hope you have all read the admirable letter of the Archbishop of Canterbury. Everybody is pleased with that letter. It
has the enormous virtue of being entirely good-humored, of trying to make peace, of avoiding making mischief — a popular
English virtue which is a credit to the English race. But it has
another English quality which is a little more questionable, and
that is the quality of being entirely anti-intellectual. The letter is
a heartfelt appeal for ambiguity.

You can imagine the Archbishop of Canterbury, if he were
continuing the controversy in private, saying to the Bishop of
Birmingham: "Now, my dear Barnes, let me recommend you
to read that wonderful book, *The Pilgrim's Progress*. Read the
history of the hero, Christian, no doubt a very splendid fellow,
and from the literary point of view the only hero of romantic
fiction resembling a real man. But he is always fighting. He is
out of one trouble into another. He is leading a terrible life.
How different to that great Peacemaker, Mr. Facing-Both-Ways!
Mr. Facing-Both-Ways has no history. Happy is the country that
has no history; and happy, you may say, is the man who has no
history; and Mr. Facing-Both-Ways in *The Pilgrim's Progress* is
that man."

Bunyan, by the way, does not even mention Mr. Facing-
Both-Ways' extraordinary historical feat of drafting the Twenty-
seventh Article of the Church of England. There being some
very troublesome people for Elizabeth to deal with — Catholics and Puritans, for instance, quarreling about Transubstantiation — Mr. Facing-Both Ways drafted an Article in two
paragraphs. The first paragraph affirmed the doctrine of Transubstantiation. The second paragraph said it was an idle superstition. Then Queen Elizabeth was able to say "Now you are all
satisfied; and you must all attend the Church of England. If you
don't, I will send you to prison."

But I am not for one moment going to debate the doctrine
of Transubstantiation. I mention it only to show, by the controversy between the Archbishop and the Bishop, that in most

debates you will find two types of mind playing with the same subject. There is one sort of mind that I think is my own sort. I sometimes call it the *Irish mind,* as distinct from the *English mind.* But that is only to make the English and Irish sit up and listen. Spengler talks not of Irish and English minds, but of the Greek, or *Grecian mind,* and the *Gothic mind* — the *Faustian mind* as he, being a German, calls it.

And in this controversy you find that what is moving Bishop Barnes is a Grecian dislike of not knowing what it is he believes, and on the other side a Gothic instinctive feeling that it is perhaps just as well not to know too distinctly.

I am not saying which is the better type of mind. I think on the whole both of them are pretty useful. But I always like to know what it is I am preaching. It gets me into trouble in England where people say, "Why go into these matters? Why do you want to think so accurately and sharply?" I can only say that my head is built that way; but I protest that I do not claim any moral superiority because when I know what I mean, the other people do not know what they mean, and very often do not know what I mean.

And one subject on which I know what I mean is the opinion which has inevitably been growing up for the last hundred years or so, not so much an opinion as a revolt against the *Misdistribution,* the obviously monstrous and anomalous Misdistribution of wealth under what we call the capitalist system.

I have always, since I got clear on the subject of Socialism, said, Don't put in the foreground the nationalization of the means of production, distribution, and exchange; you will never get there if you begin with them. You have to begin with the question of the *Distribution* of wealth.

The other day a man died, and the Government took four-and-a-half million pounds as death duty on his property. That man made all his money by the labor of men who received twenty-six shillings a week after years of qualifying for their work. Was that a reasonable distribution of wealth between them? We are all coming to the opinion that it was not reasonable.

What does Mr. Chesterton think about it?

I want to know, not only because of the public importance of his opinions, but because I have always followed Mr. Chesterton with extraordinary interest and enjoyment, and his assent to any view of mine is a great personal pleasure because I am very fond of Mr. Chesterton.

Mr. Chesterton has rejected Socialism nominally, probably because it is a rather stupid word. But he is a *Distributist,* which means today a *Re-Distributist.* He has arrived by his own path at my own position. *(Laughter.)* I do not see why you should laugh. I cannot imagine anything more natural.

But now comes the question upon which I will ask Mr. Chesterton whether he agrees with me or not. The moment I made up my mind that the present distribution of wealth was wrong, the peculiar constitution of my brain obliged me to find out exactly how far it was wrong and what is the right distribution. I went through all the proposals ever made and through the arguments used in justification of the existing distribution; and I found they were utterly insensate and grotesque. Eventually I was convinced that we ought to be tolerant of any sort of crime except unequal distribution of income.

In organized society the question always arises at what point are we justified in killing for the good of the community. I should answer in this way. If you take two shillings as your share, and another man wants two shillings and sixpence, kill him. Similarly, if a man accepts two shillings while you have two shillings and sixpence, kill him.

On the stroke of the hour, I ask Mr. Chesterton: "Do you agree with that?"

Mr. Chesterton:

Ladies and gentlemen. The answer is in the negative. I don't agree with it. Nor does Mr. Shaw. He does not think, any more than I do, that all the people in this hall, who have already created some confusion, should increase the confusion by killing each other and searching each other's pockets to see whether there is half-a-crown or two shillings in them.

As regards the general question, what I want to say is this. I should like to say, to begin with, that I have no intention of following Mr. Shaw into a discussion, which would be very improper on my part, on the condition of the Church of England. But since he has definitely challenged me on the point, I will say — he will not agree — that Mr. Shaw is indeed a peacemaker and has reconciled both sides. For if the Archbishop is anti-intellectual, there will be nobody to pretend that the Bishop is intellectual....

Voice from the Audience:

Yes he is!

Mr. Chesterton:

Now as to the much more interesting question, about a much more interesting person than Bishop Barnes — I mean Mr. Shaw — I should like to say that in a sense I can agree with him, in which case he can claim a complete victory. This is not a real controversy or debate. It is an inquiry, and I hope a profitable and interesting inquiry.

Up to a point I quite agree with him, because I did start entirely by agreeing with him, as many years ago I began by being a Socialist, just as he was a Socialist. Barring some difference of age we were in the same position. We grew in beauty side by side. I will not say literally we filled one home with glee; but I do believe we have filled a fair number of homes with glee. Whether those homes included our own personal households, it is for others to say.

But up to a point I agreed with Mr. Shaw by being a Socialist, and I agreed upon grounds he has laid down with critical justice and lucidity, grounds which I can imagine nobody being such a fool as to deny. *The distribution of property in the modern world is a monstrosity and a blasphemy.*

Thus I come to the important stage of the proceedings.

I claim that I might agree with Mr. Shaw a step farther. I have heard, from nearly all the Socialists I have known, the phrase which Mr. Shaw has with characteristic artfulness avoided, a phrase which I think everyone will agree is common to Collectivist Philosophy, and the phrase is this: *that the means of production should be owned by the community.* I ask you to note that phrase because it is really upon that that the whole question turns.

Now there is a sense in which I do agree with Mr. Bernard Shaw. There is a point up to which I would agree with that formula. So far as is possible under human conditions, I should desire the community — or, as we used to call it in the old English language, the Commons — to own the means of production. So far, I say, you have Mr. Bernard Shaw and me walking in fact side by side in the flowery meads....

But after that, alas! a change takes place. The change is owing to Mr. Shaw's vast superiority, to his powerful intellect. It is not my fault if he has remained young while I have grown in comparison wrinkled and haggard, old and experienced, and acquainted with the elementary facts of human life.

Now the first thing I want to note is this. When you say the community ought to own the means of production, what do you mean? That is the whole point. There was a time when Mr. Shaw would probably have said in all sincerity that anything possessed by the State or the Government would be in fact possessed by the Commons; in other words, by the community. I do not wish to challenge Mr. Shaw about later remarks of his, but I doubt whether Mr. Shaw, in his eternal youth, still believes in Democracy in that sense.

I quite admit he has a more hopeful and hearty outlook in some respects, and he has even gone to the length of saying that if Democracy will not do for mankind, perhaps it will do for some other creature different from mankind. He has almost proposed to invent a new animal, which might be supposed to live for 300 years. I am inclined to think that if Mr. Shaw lived for 300 years — and I heartily hope he will — I never knew a man more likely to do it — he would certainly agree with me. I would even undertake to prove it from the actual history of the last 300 years but, though I think it is probable, I will not insist upon it. As a very profound philosopher has said, "You never can tell." And it may be that Mr. Shaw's immortal power of talking nonsense would survive even that 300 years, and he would still be fixed in his unnatural theories in the matter.

Now I do not believe myself that Mr. Shaw thinks that the community — in the sense of that State which owns and rules the thing that issues postage stamps and provides policemen — I do not believe he thinks that that community is now, at this moment, identical with the Commons, and I do not believe he really thinks that in his own socialistic State it would be identical.

I am glad, therefore, that he has sufficient disordered common sense to perceive that, as a matter of fact, when you have vast systems, however just and however reasonably controlled, indirectly, by elaborate machinery of officials and other things, you do in fact find that those who rule are the few. It may be a good thing or a bad thing, but it is not true that all the people directly control.

Collectivism has put all their eggs in one basket. I do not think that Mr. Shaw believes, or that anybody believes, that 12,000,000 men, say, carry the basket, or look after the basket, or have any real distributed control over the eggs in the basket. I believe that it is controlled from the center by a few people. They may be quite right or quite necessary. A certain limit to that sort of control any sane man will recognize as necessary: it is not the same as the Commons controlling the means of production. It is a few oligarchs or a few officials who do in fact control all the means of production.

What Mr. Shaw means is, not that all the people should control the means of production, but that the product should be distributed among the vast mass of the Commons, and that is quite a different thing. It is not controlling the means of production at all. If all the citizens had simply an equal share of the income of the State they would not have any control of the capital.

That is where G. K. Chesterton differs from George Bernard Shaw. I begin at the other end. I do not think that a community arranged on the principles of Distributism and on nothing else would be a perfect community. All admit that the society that we propose is more a matter of proportion and arrangement than a perfectly clear system in which all production is pooled and the result given out in wages.

But what I say is this. Let us, so far as is possible in the complicated affairs of humanity, put into the hands of the Commons the control of the means of production — and real control. The man who owns a piece of land controls it in a direct and real sense. He really owns the means of production.

It is the same with a man who owns a piece of machinery. He can use it or not use it. Even a man who owns his own tools or works in his own workshop, to that extent owns and controls the means of production.

But if you establish right in the middle of the State one enormous machine, if you turn the handle of that machine, and somebody, who must be an official, and therefore a ruler, distributes to everybody equally the food or whatever else is produced by that machine, no single one of any of these people receiving more than any other single person, but all equal fragments — that fulfils a definite ideal of equality, yet no single one of those citizens has any control over the means of production.

They have no control whatever — unless you think that the prospect of voting about once every five years for Mr. Vanboodle — then a Socialist member — with the prospect that he will or will not make a promise to a political assembly or that he will or will not promise to ask a certain question which may or may not be answered — unless you think that by this means they possess control.

I have used the metaphor of the Collectivists of having all your eggs in one basket. Now there are men whom we are pleased to call "bad eggs." They are not all of them in politics. On the other hand, there are men who deserve the encomium of "good egg." There are, in other words, a number of good men and a number of bad men scattered among the commonwealth.

To put the matter shortly, I might say that all this theory of absolutely equal mechanical distribution depends upon a sort of use of the passive mood. It is easy enough to say Property should be distributed, but *Who* is, as it were, the subject of the verb? *Who* or *What* is to distribute? Now it is based on the idea that the Central Power which condescends to distribute will be permanently just, wise, sane, and representative of the conscience of the community which has created it. That is what we doubt.

We say there ought to be in the world a great mass of scattered powers, privileges, limits, points of resistance, so that the mass of the Commons may resist tyranny. And we say that there is a permanent possibility of that central direction, however much it may have been appointed to distribute money equally, becoming a tyranny.

I do not think it would be difficult to suggest a way in which it could happen. As soon as any particular mob of people are behaving in some way which the Governing Group chooses to regard as anti-civic, supplies could be cut off easily with the approval of this governing group. You have only to call someone by some name like *Bolshevist* or *Papist*. You have only to tie some label on a set of people, and the community will contentedly see these people starved into surrender.

We say the method to be adopted is the other method. We admit, frankly, that our method is in a sense imperfect, and only in that sense illogical. It is imperfect, or illogical, because it corresponds to the variety and differences of human life.

Mr. Shaw is making abstract diagrams of triangles, squares. and circles; we are trying to paint a portrait, the portrait of a man. We are trying to make our lines and colors follow the characteristics of the real object. Man desires certain things. He likes a certain amount of liberty, certain kinds of ownership, certain kinds of local affection, and won't be happy without them.

There are a great many other things that might be said, but I think it will be clearer if I repeat some of the things we have already said.

I do in that sense accept the propositions that the community should own the *means of production*, but I say that the Commons should own the means of production, and the only way to do that is to keep actual hold upon land.

Mr. Bernard Shaw proposes to distribute wealth. We propose to distribute power.

Mr. Shaw:

I cannot say that Mr. Chesterton has succeeded in forcing a difference of opinion on me.

There are, I suppose, at least some people in this room who have heard me orating on this platform at lectures of the Fabian Society, and they must have been considerably amused at Mr. Chesterton's attempt to impress upon me what income is.

My main activity as an economist of late has been to try to concentrate the attention of my party on the fact not only that they must distribute income, but that there is nothing else to distribute.

We must be perfectly clear as to what Capital is. I will tell you. Capital is spare money. And, of course, spare money means spare food. If I happen to have more of the means of subsistence than I can use, I may take that part that is unconsumed, and say to another man, "Let me feed you while you produce some kind of contraption that will facilitate my work in future."

But when the man has produced it for me, the Capital has all gone; there is nothing left for me or him to eat. If he has made me a spade, I cannot eat that spade.

I have said I may employ my spare subsistence in this way; but I must employ it so because it will not keep; if nobody eats it, it will go rotten. The only thing to be done with it is to have it promptly consumed. All that remains of it then is a figure in a ledger.

Some of my Capital was employed in the late war; and this country has still my name written down as the proprietor of the Capital they blew to pieces in that war.

Having said that for your instruction, let us come down to facts.

Mr. Chesterton has formed the Distributist League which organized this meeting. What was the very first thing the League said must be done? It said the coal mines must be nationalized. Instead of saying that the miner's means of production must be made his own property, it was forced to advocate making national property of the coal mines. These coal mines, when nationalized, will not be managed by the House of Commons; if they were, you would very soon have no coal. But neither will they be managed by the miners. If you ask the man working in the mine to manage the mine, he will say, "Not me, governor! That is your job."

I would like Mr. Chesterton to consider what he understands by the *means of production*. He has spoken of them in rather a nineteenth-century manner. He has been talking as though the means of production were machines.

I submit to you that the real means of production in this country are men and women, and that consequently you always have the maximum control of the individual over the means of production because it means self-control over his own person. But he must surrender that control to the Manager of the Mine because he does not know how to manage it himself.

Under the present capitalistic system he has to surrender it to the manager appointed by the Proprietors of the Mine. Under

Socialism he would have to surrender it to the manager appointed by the Coalmaster General. That would not prevent the product of the mine being equally distributed among the people.

There is no difficulty here.

In a sense Mr. Chesterton really does not disagree with me in this matter since he does see that, in the matter of fuel in this country, you have to come to nationalization. Fuel must be controlled equally for the benefit of all the people. Since we agreed upon that, I am not disposed to argue the matter further.

Now that Mr. Chesterton agreed that the coal mines will have to be nationalized, he will be led by the same pressure of facts to agree to the nationalization of everything else.

I have to allow for the pressure of facts because, as a playwright, I think of all problems in terms of actual men and women.

Mr. Chesterton lets himself idealize them sometimes as virtuous Peasant Proprietors and self-managing Petty Capitalists. The Capitalist and the Landlord have their own particular ways of robbing the poor, but their legal rights are quite different. It is a very direct way on the part of the Landlord. He may do exactly what he likes with the land he owns. If I own a large part of Scotland, I can turn the people off the land practically into the sea or across the sea. I can take women in childbearing and throw them into the snow and leave them there. That has been done. I can do it for no better reason than I think it is better to shoot deer on the land than allow people to live on it; they might frighten the deer.

But now compare that with the ownership of my umbrella. As a matter of fact, the umbrella I have tonight belongs to my wife; but I think she will permit me to call it mine for the purpose of the debate.

Now I have a very limited legal right to the use of that umbrella. I cannot do as I like with it. For instance, certain passages in Mr. Chesterton's speech tempted me to get up and smite him over the head with my umbrella. I may presently feel inclined to smite Mr. Belloc. But should I abuse my right to do what I like with my property — with my umbrella — in this way I should soon be made aware — possibly by Mr. Belloc's fist — that I cannot treat my umbrella as my own property in the way in which a Landlord can treat his land. I want to destroy ownership in order that possession and enjoyment may be raised to the highest point in every section of the community. That, I think, is perfectly simple.

There are points on which a Landlord, even a Scottish Landlord, and his Tenant the Crofter entirely agree. The Landlord objects to being shot at sight. The Irish Landlord used to object. His tenants sometimes took no notice of his objection, but all the same they had a very strong objection to being shot themselves.

You have no objection to a State law being carried out vigorously that people shall not shoot one another. There is no difficulty in modern civilized States in having it carried out. If you could once convince the people that inequality of income is a greater social danger than murder, very few people would want to continue to commit it; and the State could suppress it with the assent of the community generally.

We are always adding fresh crimes to the calendar. Why not enact that no person shall live in this community without pulling his weight in the social boat, without producing more than he consumes — because you have to provide for the accumulation of spare money as Capital — who does not replace by his own labor what he takes out of the community, who attempts to live idly, as men are proud to live nowadays. Is there any greater difficulty in treating such a parasite as a malefactor, than in treating a murderer as a malefactor?

Having said that much about the property part of the business, I think I have succeeded in establishing that Mr. Chesterton does not disagree with me.

I should like to say I do not believe in Democracy.

I do believe in Catholicism; but I hold that the Irish Episcopal Protestant Church, of which I was baptized a member, takes the name of Catholicism in vain; that the Roman Church has also taken it in vain; and so with the Greek Church and the rest. My Catholicism is really catholic Catholicism — that is what I believe in, as apart from this voting business and Democracy.

Does Mr. Chesterton agree with me on that?

Mr. Chesterton:

Among the bewildering welter of fallacies which Mr. Shaw has just given us, I prefer to deal first with the simplest.

When Mr. Shaw refrains from hitting me over the head with his umbrella, the real reason — apart from his real kindness of heart, which makes him tolerant of the humblest of the creatures of God — is, not because he does not own his umbrella, but because he does not own my head.

As I am still in possession of that imperfect organ, I will proceed to use it to the confutation of some of his other fallacies.

I should like to say now what I ought perhaps to have said earlier in the evening, that we are enormously grateful to Mr. Shaw for his characteristic generosity in consenting to debate with a humble movement like our own.

I am so conscious of that condescension on his part that I should feel it a very unfair return to ask him to read any of our potty little literature or cast his eye over our little weekly paper or become conscious of the facts we have stated a thousand times.

One of these facts, with which every person who knows us is familiar, is our position with regard to the coal question. We have said again and again that in our human state of society there must be a class of things called *Exceptions*. We admit that upon the whole in the very peculiar case of coal it is desirable and about the best way out of the difficulty that it should be controlled by the officials of the State, just in the same way as postage stamps are controlled.

No one says anything else about postage stamps.

I cannot imagine that anyone wants to have his own postage stamps, of perhaps more picturesque design and varied colors.

I can assure you that Distributists are perfectly sensible and sane people, and they have always recognized that there are institutions in the State in which it is very difficult to apply the principle of individual property, and that one of these cases is the discovery under the earth of valuable minerals.

Socialists are not alone in believing this.

Charles I, who, I suppose, could not be called a Socialist, pointed out that certain kinds of minerals ought to belong to the State; that is, to the Commons.

We have said over and over again that we support the nationalization of the coal mines, not as a general example of Distribution but as a commonsense admission of an Exception. The reason why we make it an Exception is because it is not very easy to see how the healthy principle of personal ownership can be applied. If it could, we should apply it with the greatest pleasure. We consider personal ownership infinitely more healthy. If there were a way in which a miner could mark out one particular piece of coal and say, "This is mine, and I am proud of it," we should have made an enormous improvement upon State management. There are cases in which it is very difficult to apply the principle, and that is one of them.

It is the reverse of the truth for Mr. Shaw to say that the logic of that fact will lead me to the application of the same principle to other cases, like the ownership of the land. One could not illustrate it better than by the case of coal. It may be true, for all I know, that if you ask a miner if he would like to manage the mine, he would say, "I do not want to manage it; it is for my betters to manage it." I had not noticed that meek and simple manner among miners. I have even heard complaints of the opposite temper in that body.

I defy Mr. Shaw to say if you went to the Irish farmers, or the French farmers, or the Serbian or the Dutch farmers, or any of the millions of Peasant owners throughout the world — I defy him to say if you went to the farmer and said, "Who controls these farms?" he would say, "It is not for the likes of me to control a farm." Mr. Shaw knows perfectly well it is nonsense to suggest that Peasants would talk that way anywhere.

It is part of his complaints against Peasants that they claim personal possessions. I am not likely to be led to the denial of property in land, for I know ordinary normal people who feel property in land to be normal.

I fully agree with Mr. Shaw, and speak as strongly as he would speak, of the abomination and detestable foulness and sin of Landlords who drove poor people from their land in Scotland and elsewhere.

It is quite true that men in possession of land have committed these crimes; but I do not see why wicked officials under a socialistic State could not commit these crimes. But that has nothing to do with the principle of ownership in land. In fact these very Highland Crofters, these very people thus abominably outraged and oppressed, if you asked them what they want, would probably say, "I want to own my own croft; I want to own my own land."

Mr. Shaw's dislike of the Landlord is not so much a denial of the right to private property, not so much that he owns the land, but that the Landlord has swallowed up Private Property. In the face of these facts of millions and millions of ordinary human beings who have Private Property, who know what it is like to own property, I must confess that I am not overwhelmed and crushed by Mr. Shaw's claim that he knows all about men and women as they really are. I think Mr. Shaw knows something about certain kinds of men and women; though he sometimes makes them a little more amusing than they really are. But I cannot agree with his discovery that Peasants do not like Peasant property because I know the reverse is the fact.

Then we come to the general point he raised about the State. He raised a very interesting question. He said that after all the

State does command respect, that we all do accept laws even though they are issued by an official group.

Up to a point I willingly accept his argument. The Distributist is certainly not an anarchist. He does not believe it would be a good thing if there were no such laws. But the reason why most of these laws are accepted is because they correspond with the common conscience of mankind. Mr. Shaw and Bishop Barnes might think it would be an inadequate way of explaining it, but we might call attention to an Hebraic code called the *Ten Commandments*. They do, I think, correspond pretty roughly to the moral code of every religion that is at all sane. These all reverence certain ideas about "Thou shalt not kill." They all have a reverence for the commandment which says, "Thou shalt not covet thy neighbor's goods." They reverence the idea that you must not covet his house or his ox or his ass. It should be noted, too, that besides forbidding us to covet our neighbor's property, this commandment also implies that every man has a right to own some property.

Mr. Shaw:

I now want to ask Mr. Chesterton why he insists on the point about the nationalization of the coal mines — on which he agrees with me — that they are an Exception. Are they an Exception? In what way are the coal mines an Exception? What is the fundamental reason why you must nationalize your coal mine? The reason is this. If you will go up to the constituency of Mr. Sidney Webb, to the Sunderland coast, you will be able to pick up coal for nothing, absolutely nothing at all. You see people doing it there. You take a perambulator, or barrow, or simple sack, and when the tide goes out, you go out on the foreshore and pick up excellent coal.

If you go to other parts of England, like Whitehaven, you will find you have to go through workings driven out under the sea, which took twenty years to make, twenty years continual expenditure of capital before coal could be touched, where men going down the shaft have to travel sometimes two or three miles to their work.

That is the reason at bottom why you cannot distribute your coal mine. The reason you have to pay such monstrous prices for your coal is they are fixed by the cost of making the submarine mines. People who have mines like the Sunderland foreshore naturally make colossal fortunes. Everyone can see at once that in order to have any kind of equable dealing in coal, the only way is to charge the citizens the average cost for the total national supply. You cannot average the cost by putting your eggs into different baskets.

Now this is not the Exception — it is the Rule. You have exactly the same difference in the case of the land. You have land worth absolutely nothing at all and land worth a million an acre or more. And the acre worth more than a million and the acre worth nothing are within half-an-hour's drive in a taxi. You cannot say that the coal mine is an Exception.

The coal mine is only one instance. Mr. Chesterton in arriving at the necessity for the nationalization of the coal mines has started on his journey toward the nationalization of all the industries. If he goes on to the land, and from the land to the factory, and from there to every other industrial department, he will find that every successive case is an Exception; and eventually he will have to say to himself, "I think it will be better to call nationalization the Rule rather than the Exception."

I must deny that I ever said that the coal miner says he wants to be ruled by his betters. I may not be a Democrat, but I am not a snob. Intellectually, I am a snob, and you will admit that I have good ground for that. Socially, I am not a snob. There is no question of betters at all in the matter. The Manager is not better than the Executant, nor the Executant better than the Manager. Both are equally necessary and equally honorable. But if you ask the Executant to manage, he will refuse on the ground that it is not his job; and vice versa.

Mr. Chesterton says he does not see why State officials under a system which recognizes nationalization of land should not act as the old Landlords acted. I should say, in the first place, they won't have the power. A State official does what he is instructed to do and paid to do, just as a Landlord's Agent does; and there is no more danger of the official making himself a Landlord than there is now of the Agent making himself one.

As to the instinct of owning — and you have it widely in the country — you have not got it in the towns. People are content to live in houses they do not own. When they possess them, they often find them a great nuisance. But you must not conclude that because a miner would refuse to manage a mine, a farmer will refuse to manage his farm. The farmer is himself a Manager.

How does this wonderful system of Peasant proprietorship work? Do you realize that it has to be broken up every day? The reason is that when a man owning a farm has a family, each son, when the farmer dies, has a right to an equal part of the land. They find that this arrangement is entirely impossible, and they have to make some other arrangement, and some of the sons have to go off into the towns to work. It is unthinkable that all could remain on the land; you cannot split up the land and give every person a bit of property....

I have stolen two minutes from Mr. Chesterton, and I apologize.

Mr. Chesterton:

I am sure Mr. Shaw is very welcome to as many minutes as I can offer him, or anything else, for his kindness in entertaining us this evening.

It is rather late now, and there is not much time left for me.

He has been rather slow in discovering what Distributism is and what the whole question is about. If this were the beginning of the discussion, I could do over our system completely. I could tell him exactly what we think about property in towns.

It is absurd to say it does not exist. In rural ownership different problems have to be faced. We are not cutting a thing up into mathematical squares. We are trying to deal with human beings, creatures quite outside the purview of Mr. Shaw and his political philosophy.

We know town people are a little different from country people; business of one kind is different from business of another kind; difficulties arise about family, and all the rest of it. We show man's irrepressible desire to own property and because some Landlords have been cruel, it is no use talking of abolishing, denying, and destroying property, saying no one shall have any property at all.

It is characteristic of his school, of his age. The morality he represents is above all the morality of negations. Just as it says you must not drink wine at all as the only solution to a few people drinking too much; just as it would say you must not touch meat or smoke tobacco at all.

Let us always remember, therefore, that when Mr. Shaw says he can persuade all men to give up the sentiment of Private Property, it is in exactly the same hopeful spirit that he says he will get all of you to give up meat, tobacco, beer, and a vast number of other things.

He will not do anything of the sort, and I suspect he himself suspects by this time that he will not do it.

It is quite false to say you must have a centralized machinery, even in towns. It is quite false to say that all forces must be used, as they are in monopolies, from the center. It is absurd to say that because the wind is a central thing, you cannot separate windmills. How am I to explain all that in five minutes?

I could go through a vast number of fallacies into which he has fallen. He said, ironically, he would like to see me go down a mine. I have no difficulty in imagining myself sinking in such a fashion in any geological deposit. I really should like to see him doing work on a farm because he would find out about five hundred pieces of nonsense he has been speaking to be the nonsense they are.

It is absolutely fallacious to suggest that there is some sort of difficulty in Peasantries whereby they are bound to disappear. The answer to that is that they have not disappeared. It is part of the very case against Peasantry, among those who do not like them, that they are antiquated, covered with hoary superstition. Why have they remained through all these centuries if they must immediately break up and become impossible? There is an answer to all that, and I am quite prepared to give it at some greater length than five minutes.

But at no time did I say that we must make the whole community a community of agricultural Peasants. It is absurd. What I said was that a desire for property which is universal, everywhere, does appear in a perfect and working example in the ownership of land.

It only remains for me to say one thing.

Mr. Shaw said, in reference to the State owning the means of production, that men and women are the only means of production. I quite accept the parallel of the phrase. His proposition is that the government, the officials of the State, should own the men and women; in other words, that the men and women should be slaves.

Mr. Belloc:

I was told when I accepted this onerous office that I was to sum up.

I shall do nothing of the sort.

In a very few years from now this debate will be antiquated.

I will now recite you a poem.

> Our civilization
> Is built upon coal.
> Let us chant in rotation
> Our civilization

That lump of damnation
Without any soul,
Our civilization
Is built upon coal.

In a very few years,
It will float upon oil.
Then give three hearty cheers,
In a very few years
We shall mop up our tears
And have done with our toil.
In a very few years
It will float upon oil.

I do not know how many years — five, ten, twenty — this debate will be as antiquated as crinolines are.

I am surprised that neither of the two speakers pointed out that one of three things is going to happen.

One of three things — not one of two.

It is always one of three things.

This industrial civilization which, thank God, oppresses only the small part of the world in which we are most inextricably bound up, will break down, and, therefore, end from its monstrous wickedness, folly, ineptitude, leading to a restoration of sane, ordinary human affairs, complicated but based as a whole upon the freedom of the citizens.

Or it will break down and lead to nothing but a desert.

Or it will lead the mass of men to become contented slaves, with a few rich men controlling them.

Take your choice.

You will all be dead before any of the three things comes off.

One of the three things is going to happen, or a mixture of two, or possibly a mixture of the three combined.

Murders: reference to Chesterton's popular mystery stories with a Catholic priest, Father Brown, as the sleuthhound; fifty-one short stories published in five volumes (1911, 1914, 1926, 1927, 1935).

Plays: reference to the more than two dozen plays GBS had written by the time of this debate; among them, *Mrs. Warren's Profession, Man and Superman, Pygmalion,* and *Saint Joan. Of late years...I have almost been reverenced:* GBS was awarded the Nobel Prize for Literature in 1925. *Archbishop of Canterbury:* Randall Thomas Davidson (1848–1930), who held the See of Canterbury from 1903 to 1928. *Bishop of Birmingham:* Earnest William Barnes (1874–1953), a pacifist who attacked ritualistic practices and promoted a scientific approach to Christian dogma that brought him into conflict with his fellow bishops. *Pilgrim's Progress:* dream allegory, first published in 1678, by Puritan John Bunyan (1628–88), that has become a classic devotional work in all Christian denominations; GBS called it "flawless as an ethical, religious, social, and literary guide to conduct and as an image of the human pilgrimage toward redemption" (AH, 25). *Twenty-seventh Article of the Church of England:* that one of the Thirty-nine Articles of Religion, doctrines of the Church of England formulated in 1571 and affirmed by its clergy upon their ordination, dealing with Baptism as a "sign of profession," "mark of difference," "Regeneration or New Birth." *Transubstantiation:* one of several explanations of just how the substance (though not the appearance) of the bread and wine in the Eucharist becomes Christ's body and blood; first termed so in the twelfth century; this explanation is favored by Roman Catholics, disfavored by Anglicans and Puritans. *Oswald Spengler* (1880–1936): German philosopher whose once-influential reputation rested entirely on his two-volume work, *The Decline of the West* (1918–22). *Faustian mind:* reminiscent of the mind of German Johann Faust (1488–1541), a wandering astrologer and necromancer who was reputed to have sold his soul to the Devil. *Grecian dislike:* reference to the altar the Apostle Paul found on the Areopagus, a hill north of the Acropolis; it was dedicated to the "Unknown God"; Athenians lusted to know that God's identity; Paul told them (Acts 17:19–23). *Distributist:* member of the Distributist League, which advocated the distribution of land and encouraged property owning so that men could have a hedge against exploitation and inflation; ideally, every man was to be his own employer. *Eternal youth:* in 1928, the time of the debate, GBS was seventy-two, and GKC was fifty-four. *Distributist League:* sponsor of the debate, it proposed the redistribution of power. *To smite Mr. Belloc / Mr. Belloc's fist:* in previous years Shaw created a ferocious monster — really a four-legged pantomime elephant, Belloc the fore-legs, Chesterton, the hind — whom he branded "Chesterbelloc"; its major crime had been Chesterton's illustrating ten of Belloc's forgettable novels; their minor crimes in favor of Distributism and against Fabianism continued to the day of this debate (MFF, 75). *Crofter:* Scottish subsistence farmer or small-holder whose house and land were known as his croft. *Charles I* (1600–1649): king of Great Britain and Ireland (1625–49); his authoritarian rule and quarrels with Parliament provoked a civil war that led to his execution. *Sidney Webb* (1859–1947), Baron Passfield: with his wife Beatrice (1858–1943), early and dominant members of the Fabian Society and co-founders of the London School of Economics and Political Science. *Sunderland coast:* port city on the northeast coast of England with river Wear flowing into the North Sea. *Perambulator:* baby carriage. *Whitehaven:* town on the coast of Cumbria in northwest England. *Meat, tobacco, beer:* GBS was a vigorous but happy abstainer from meat, tobacco, beer, and other simple pleasures. *Source: Do We Agree?* (London: Distributist League, 1928); as it appears in CW11, 539–60.

THE LAST WORD

PUTTING HUMPTY-DUMPTY
BACK TOGETHER

Who won? Who won that debate entitled "Do We Agree?"
Well, who knows?

Chesterton's followers thought he did. Shaw's supporters
thought he did. The Distributists were happy on the one side,
and the Fabians on the other. Nonpartisans, if there were any,
probably thought it was a draw. Of course, neither debater
really won, and the arguments of neither one prevailed with the
English government then or since. To this day England's vast
wealth remains undistributed. That's what would make both
Chesterton and Shaw very sad indeed.

We in the next century, upon reading the transcript of "Do
We Agree?" for the first time, may also ask the same question.
Who won?

The arguments for Chesterton's distributism seem about as
good as Shaw's arguments against it. Belloc thought it a draw;
but, clown that he was, his openers and closers-cum-poem
trumped both of the speakers.

"Little could anyone that night in the Kingsway Hall know
it," wrote biographer Joseph Pearce, "but Belloc, in ringing
down the curtain of the debate, was also ringing down the
curtain on the Distributist League" (JP, 327).

Which raises another question.

If Chesterton didn't win this one, how many did he win? All, most, some, none? That may very well be a false question.

Perhaps the real question should be, Did Chesterton have to win all, most, some, none?

Many readers then as now have considered him a champion, departing every dawn breathing fire in front of him and returning every dusk dragging a dead Saracen behind him. But to read him as a champion who never lost is to misread him; to put more pressure on his heritage and his writings than they should be required to bear.

As for "champion," at least in Chesterton's case, the term would better be defined as "a knight who showed up for battle every day, no matter how ragged his performance the day before."

Chesterton has been, and continues to be, attractive to all Christians, whether rigid Conservative Evangelicals or raving Roman Catholics, denominations who professedly find each other's company unpleasant, to say the very least.

But virtuous people are like that. They're living reproofs to the narrowness, the exclusiveness, of the rest of us. At the same time they're the best proofs that God exists — quirky and quarky as that God may be.

Paradoxy, Humility, Hilarity — these three virtues make a lovely bouquet for a Christian. But for an intellectual and imaginative Christian, they're a downright necessity.

As if a proof of their bouquet were necessary, they continue to generate a sweet spiritual generosity toward those who think, imagine, and pray otherwise.

Only a fool would say we'll never see Chesterton's like again.

Everyone got along quite nicely before he came, and normalcy has certainly returned since he left.

Or has it?

All we have to do is look around.

He is us, and we are him.

Even if we don't pick him out of a crowd right away, other people will mistake us for him as soon as we open our mouths.

It's the speaking of God with hilarity in our hearts and on our lips that gives us away.

Not that there's anything wrong with that.

Acknowledgments

Philip Yancey. John Wilson. Mark Riley. Troy Thibodeaux. John Williams. Marjorie Lamp Mead at The Wade Center, Wheaton College. Martin Ward for the G. K. Chesterton Web Page. Dale Ahlquist for The American Chesterton Society Web Page.